T0110914

WHISPERING
OF THE
LIGHT

*A life journey full of faith, hope, courage,
perseverance, healing, adventures, and magic*

PAVEENA POSANG, M.D.

BALBOA.PRESS

A DIVISION OF HAY HOUSE

Balboa Press books may be ordered through booksellers or by contacting:

Balboa Press
A Division of Hay House
1663 Liberty Drive
Bloomington, IN 47403
www.balboapress.com
844-682-1282

Because of the dynamic nature of the Internet, any web addresses or
links contained in this book may have changed since publication and
may no longer be valid. The views expressed in this work are solely those
of the author and do not necessarily reflect the views of the publisher,
and the publisher hereby disclaims any responsibility for them.

The author of this book does not dispense medical advice or prescribe the use
of any technique as a form of treatment for physical, emotional, or medical
problems without the advice of a physician, either directly or indirectly. The
intent of the author is only to offer information of a general nature to help
you in your quest for emotional and spiritual well-being. In the event you use
any of the information in this book for yourself, which is your constitutional
right, the author and the publisher assume no responsibility for your actions.

Any people depicted in stock imagery provided by Getty Images are
models, and such images are being used for illustrative purposes only.
Certain stock imagery © Getty Images.

Print information available on the last page.

ISBN: 979-8-7652-2898-2 (sc)
ISBN: 979-8-7652-2897-5 (hc)
ISBN: 979-8-7652-2896-8 (e)

Library of Congress Control Number: 2022909088

Balboa Press rev. date: 05/16/2022

This magical story must be told!

Acknowledgments

There are so many people to thank for being there for me throughout my lifetime and for bringing the brightest light into my soul's journey.

I am thankful for my husband, who is my best friend. He has been there for me through thick and thin and has never given up on me for thirty-four years. He has picked me up from life situations that have brought me to my knees. He continues to lift me up daily.

I am thankful for my grandparents, mom, aunts, uncles, and family. My Aunt Sue, mom's youngest sister, has done so much for me and my entire family. Aunt Sue, with her heart of gold and with relentless determination in her spirit, has fought head-on and won many of life's battles. Her success in life, including becoming a physician, has lifted the life of our family's future generations to the next level.

Our Aunt Somboon, mom's oldest sister, came and rescued us while we were in Bangkok and had nowhere else to go. Our grandparents took us in. They are no longer with us in person, but their spirits continue to guide us and remind us to do the right thing and always to move forward in life.

I can still hear the sound of the train that took us to our grandparents. Mom could not afford enough train tickets, so I slept under the seat. It surely was the ride to our new beginning.

Mom is my forever hero! Earth has chosen the strongest mom to bring us life. She raised us with the purest love and guided us with the wisdom of a warrior.

I am thankful for my brother and two sisters. All four of us are in health care—two physicians and two doctors of pharmacy. I was diagnosed with lupus and could not walk due to total body swelling and pain at age nineteen while in college. I was told to give up college, but instead I did not show up for the treatment. I went on and graduated from nursing school, then from medical school, to help more people. I thank God for taking away my illness without medical treatment. I thank God for guiding all four of us to excel in our lives and careers in health care. We are now able to help the world with our gifts of healing.

I am thankful for the many in my soul family and great friends who have been there for me. They love me unconditionally without judgment, and they pointed me in the right directions when I was blinded from life's crises. I am forever in debt to all my compassionate teachers and professors who spent countless hours teaching me not only new knowledge as a tool to survive my career, but about life itself.

I still thank God daily for sending me my high school English teacher, Sharon Paxton. She spent extra time teaching me to read and write English so I could have success in my life and career by having the ability and the power to communicate in this new land that is now home.

I cannot go on without thanking this next important person in my life. One of my best friends whom I have known for more than twenty years, Jim Behmer, has always been my English consultant. He kindly proofread everything important that I have written over the years. His background as an engineer who loves to read all kinds of books, and his kind heart, made him my best English consultant.

I am thankful for all my patients over the past twenty-plus years who trusted in me and allowed me to care for their health. I am honored that they chose me to be their care provider. I dearly miss many of them and continue to cherish all the memories in my heart and soul. I still speak to the spirits of the wonderful patients that I have lost over the years as I remember their beautiful love for life and for their families.

I surrender to my divine team, the higher power, the spirits of my ancestors, and the source of my life force energy, the light of my soul. This team continues to guide me and protect me as I keep moving forward with my life's mission and writing this book. I was guided by the power of love to write this book. May the angel's light within this book bring brightness, inspiration, healing, and magic to all of you as you read it.

Contents

Dr. Paveena Posang's letter to the readers

I am writing this message from the ink that is spilling from my heart and soul. My burning wish is to prepare you for the exciting journey of your life. Life is really a journey for a quest of your own truth and of your dreams. I hope that some of my experiences will be your inspiration, a road map or a compass to help you get to your destination without getting lost or delayed.

I hope that my words and my inner light will be with you and keep you company even if I may not be here on this beautiful earth one day. I hope that you will sail through your life's journey, floating and enjoying the rocking of little waves. I hope that you will find enough waves that your boat of life will rock and sooth you to comfort. I hope all of you can avoid the big destructive waves that can wreck your boat and keep you away from your destination.

I learn every day from life experiences, everything and everybody around me. When you keep an open mind, it is like throwing out a big net into the sea; you will catch both big fish and little fish. You may even catch the hidden treasures from the deep sea. It is then for you to decide what you will keep or adapt as your strategies for life. You will have more choices and support. However, don't forget that little fish or little things in life can be so colorful and beautiful. Other people's life stories and their experiences can be your earth teacher, motivation, inspiration, and strength.

I hope that my own light instilled in this book will support you and light your passion and your path if you ever are faced with a dark night of your soul's journey. I wish all of you many blessings and success in all areas of your life's missions. I see myself not as a wounded old soul, but a survivor of life.

I live life daily with the highest gratitude in my heart for each small thing in life. My heart and soul are forever in debt for the guidance and the magic of the higher being and my divine team that have saved my life countless times. I am forever grateful for so many wonderful people who had never given up on me. All of you know who you are because you are my soul family. I am at peace as a human being on this earth walking on the path of my destiny from the beginning of my life until the last life chapter before my blissful soul goes on to the next assignment.

This magical story must be told!

I know that some of you out there (despite your different background, cultures, or religions) have had dreams, visions, premonitions, or certain unusual life experiences that were very vivid and real. Some of you may have had magical or mystical experiences that you cannot explain, but which felt very real and personal to you. Some of you may recall some bizarre coincidences or supernatural events that have forever impacted your life or saved you from possible death. When your mortal experiences merged with the divine, the experiences become mystical in nature and those experiences brought you closer to the infinite divine intellect. Some of you can relate to me and my story that I am about to tell you.

A story is always a story. You may choose to listen and read about it, but you are not obligated to believe it! I hope this story will at least entertain you and inspire your spirit to live life to the fullest during your lifetime. I hope that you will gain insight and understanding into the magic of your own life that will continue to unfold day after day. I hope my story will bring awareness of your tremendous inner forces and prior soul wisdom or soul experiences locked up deep inside you. You can benefit by bringing these inner forces out in action as your power to fight and continue living as a human. These could be your life solutions, answers, or battle-of-life strategies that you can hear as *they whisper in your silence* or your intuition. I want to stir and awaken your soul to live to your magnificent potential.

I hope my story will encourage or ignite your passion to continue the pursuit of your happiness until you reach enlightenment or have deeper understanding of the truth of your own callings, your destinies, or your life's missions. I would like to ask you to keep your hopes and the pursuits of all your dreams going and to never quit living your beautiful life. You must continue to keep the aspirations to fulfill your ambition. Please never stop the discovery of the truth of your own life and continue the deep love of being alive as a human.

We are never alone, and we must call for help from our divine team or our higher power. We have the team of cosmic light including our guardian angels, our spirit guides, our higher selves, and spirits of our ancestors with us to help guide and protect us throughout our entire lifetime. You will hear their messages as the *whispering of their light* as they communicate through the gate of your intuition.

There is a voice inside us that calls to us or nags us even more obviously and loudly when we are in danger to pay attention to our intuition, messages, signs, or synchronicity. It tells us to read the signs, interpret our dreams, and follow our gut feelings. Your support team from the universe and your divine team never give up on you as your light (your soul or life force energy) is also a part of their cosmic light. Your divine team will forever be your never-giving-up allies in the battles of life.

We are all connected as one. We have our higher selves, our intuition, embedded with many lifetimes of soul wisdom or soul memories that communicate openly with our divine team. This flow of communication connects to or speaks to us even though we may choose not to listen. Every answer that you seek will come when you silence your mind and listen to your own divine teams and your own higher selves.

The answers to your own life are all there for you. You don't need to look far in the distance for the solution that may end up being the distraction that may cause you to make a detour in your life's journey. The solutions that were given to us by our divine teams are all the best way. They are peaceful, harmonious, sensible, purposeful, truthful, and effective.

Sometimes the solution given seems odd at that moment of our life's journey. The future will reveal the true purpose or lesson in life through the chaotic or complete confusion orchestrated by the given solution. Many times in life we have to look back to understand or recapture the purpose.

We all accepted or were given a set of life missions before we even came into this life. We must complete them and reach enlightenment or the finish line once our missions have been fulfilled. We have the absolute power of free will as humans, which many times can get us in trouble if we choose to go off our paths or let ourselves step into disharmony. Some missions take multiple lifetimes to complete.

Once we achieve the goals of our life paths before the final destination, we will reach the higher understanding of ourselves. We will have new insight and perception of ourselves. We will clearly see the true purpose of our whole lives. We will start putting them into action with unwavering determination, using all the knowledge we have gained from previous completed steps toward the countdown of our destination or our life's last chapters. Once we reach that set point (set by the divine team and known as divine's timing), we will gain a collection of significant life experiences that will cause a total shift of our cores or our existence on earth as humans to become a body of wisdom or knowledge.

Life is truly a journey to train, create, evolve, transform, grow, expand, renew, stabilize, program, improve, or invent us to become warriors of life. You will eventually learn to accept who you truly are in your own given magnificent power so that you will embrace self-worth and self-love. You will learn to commit to yourself first and realize that you are enough and most important.

You will awaken to the idea that you deserve your own love. You need no one else to feel happy or fulfilled. You will learn that you are already the body of love and light. You do not have to search the whole world for it. You will begin saying, "I am so happy to be me and to stay being me!" You will learn that you need no one else's approval, just your own, to feel loved, important, or beautiful. You will be empowered to be an authentic you who can speak and stand in your own truth. You will no longer feel neglected or like a victim. You will finally realize that it is a choice. *You hold the absolute power to feel loved, respected, and accepted and to experience joy.* You will begin housecleaning as the light starts to shine and you can see clearly. You will start cleaning out things that will no longer serve you and your higher purpose including situations, thoughts, things, and even people. Your rose-tinted glasses will be broken, and your naked eyes will see the world as it is. My mind hears the song by Jimmy Cliff: "I can see clearly now the rain is gone. I can see all obstacles in my way. Gone are the dark clouds that had me blind. It's gonna be a bright, bright sunshiny day." There will be less shadow or darkness in the vision field of your life.

No matter how many times you were beaten by others, you will not forget; however, your life warrior's heart will begin to forgive. Forgiveness will start by forgiving yourself. You will understand that all humans are beautiful light having human experiences. Once your heart has expelled all the pain, hurts, sadness, disappointment, regrets, and grudges, peace will take over your heart and soul.

Peace will bring with it tremendous power for growth, joy, fulfillment, balance, creativity, inspiration, happiness, and the most important—the ability to forgive more easily.

These combined emotions of your higher self may feel unfamiliar. You have forgotten the blissful feeling of your true life that had been embedded all along deep in your ancient and immortal soul.

We will be guided to awaken once all of life's experiences have decorated our souls with accomplishment and strength during our current lifetime. I hope that my story will awaken people earlier and help them gain the necessary insight to stop delaying. Then you can reach the finish line earlier before your physical bodies wilt away. Our soul memories will collect strength through soul experiences of many lifetimes. Our life will bring challenges or missions until you have completed all of them. Don't forget that some of the same challenges will be presented to us the second time or multiple times as a test to see whether we have learned our lessons from the past. The immortal light within you will then go on to create more soul journeys in different lifetimes or different dimensions.

Your thoughts, combined with the power from your divine team, are mighty forces that can manifest anything in the mortal world. Thoughts truly become things! Happy, joyful, and positive thoughts will manifest those qualities in your life. The secret of manifestation is to have a true intention combined with unwavering faith that your divine team is there to help. This is the most important lesson we must master early as a human being since we already hold a power of manifesting life within our matrix. This must be taught early to our children so they will grow and be the supermanifestors of their own destinies to lead successful lives.

I was awakened from life by my divine team as a human to my mission in this lifetime by the flowing of their messages, which I call *"whispering of the light."* I started to see the numbers 111 and 1111, often in repeating sequences, everywhere after I joined the US Air Force in 2010. I was stationed for four years at Langley Air Force Base in Hampton (now Joint Base Langley-Eustis), Virginia, as a military physician with the rank of lieutenant colonel. I started to wake up and see 111 on my alarm clock. I would pay for groceries and the receipts either came out $11.11 or $111. At certain times, I felt something in my mind like an inner voice alerting me to look at the clock when the time was 1:11 or 11:11. I would check my patients' blood sugar and other lab tests and they would come out 111. Or their blood pressure systolic reading would be 111, their heart rate 111, or their weight would be calculated by the computer from pounds to kilograms as 111.11. I intermittently experienced what I call "download" especially before I slept or when I awakened from sleep. For a few minutes, I saw small, linear lights flashing in my vision while my eyes were closed.

These happened too frequently to be coincidences. In 2019, I started seeing golden letters floating in my vision, similar to the hieroglyphs in ancient Egypt. I knew that a power on another dimension was trying to communicate with me and change my vibration or my energy field or composition by the power instilled within these ancient hieroglyphs.

One day I was taking a nap. I was half awake as I felt the presence of someone standing at the top of my head. I thought the body was my husband. I reached up my hands toward the top of my head without looking. Suddenly a very bright light like the light from a lightning bolt quickly entered my physical body. I saw beautiful, small bright lights as they exploded throughout the room. The brightness and the powerful glare blinded me for a second. As I looked up to the top of my head, there was a beautiful and brilliant large silvery white body. Somehow my heart felt safe without fear of the friendly body of light.

After a few more years, I started calling the healing light from this beautiful body my *"angel's light, the light of an ascending master of light."* For two days after the light emerged within my physical body, my hearing became unusually very clear and keen. I could hear the birds talking to me from far away. I had the habit of setting out bird feed, especially during the winter months. I somehow understood the appreciation from the birds in their melodious sounds. The trees, the soft wind, and the sunshine started to have sounds as if they were trying to communicate with me, and I became more connected with Mother Earth and nature.

I would awaken from my sleep with my phone playing a video talking about "light worker." I had never heard of this term before, since I had spent my life exploring and studying modern medicine. I discovered later that a light worker, according to Urban Dictionary.com, is a person who was placed on this earth for a reason. Their reason for being placed on earth is to bring light wherever they go. Every light worker usually had a very rough upbringing. They had experienced trauma and hurt. This trauma and hurt were simply their training for their destinies.

To understand the way out of the darkness, one must live in the darkness. Light workers experience life in the darkness. Unfortunately, some do not always find their way out due to addiction, suicide, and mental illness. Every potential light worker hears the call for duty. Their intuition will let them know that they have a serious duty here on earth. Some listen, some ignore. Those who listen must first heal themselves. Once they are completely healed and spiritually whole, they can help others. Light workers will save the world in the darkest of times. They know the way out. They will never stop working toward positive change, spiritual growth, and a society that is far less shallow and a lot more loving. Light workers are the people you feel pulled toward; they are the people you take advantage of if you happen to be a user. Beware, though ... they never allow disloyalty for long. Their growth game is strong. They are the future of this world.[1] Many of you may by now have realized that you are a light worker.

Several more unusual or mystical experiences started happening to me. I would awaken from sleep seeing myself with well-kept, thick black shoulder-length hair, and a face that was not mine. My intuition said that it was me wearing an ancient Egyptian headpiece and a flowing white dress. The headpiece was put together with multiple small rectangular shapes alternated in gold and deep green colors into the shape of a pyramid. Despite my being awake and in full awareness of my body, I felt the wind blowing the light cloth dress on my skin as I walked or moved around.

I started to attract butterflies at the last moment of their life cycle. For some unknown reason, they flew and dropped dead in front of me. I picked some up in my hand, and they began to wake up. They flew away after spending a few minutes in my palm. I felt electric sensations as if the butterflies were pulling from me the angel's light that they needed. Some of the butterflies did not fly away. They started flapping their wings again for several minutes before their lives ended. I was alert and awakened to my calling and life's purpose, to help others with my angel's light.

One day a video started to play. It was Frankie, a lady in her seventies in Ashville, North Carolina. Frankie was a born empath (an individual with special psychic and empathic abilities who can sense the emotions and feelings of others). She is also a clairvoyant (a person with ability to perceive events in the future), and a clairaudient (a person with the ability to hear sounds beyond the reach of ordinary person). Frankie spends most of her life helping people communicate with their spirit guides, so I called and spoke to her.

I told Frankie that I was guided by the higher power to talk to her. She said, "Yes, your ascending master of light prepared your space by changing your vibration/energy field before stepping into your personal physical space. You need to wake up and start to learn how to use your light to help humanity. The light and your DNA work together to bring healing to others. You were born with the DNA of a healer."

I was guided to take quantum touch and Reiki classes as the modalities to help me present angel's light to others. It took me another two years to train to master teacher level of Reiki and I attended quantum touch training as well. I started to incorporate angel's light within my family medicine practice, as I generally already minimize the use of modern medications that often have side effects.

I tried to make time to spend a few minutes at the end of my patients' visits to instill angel's light to support the healing process of those who were open to receive it. I normally asked my patients if they would like their energy reset.

I would call the angel's light with my mind and then set the intention for the light to support each patient's highest good while touching the top of patient's head. I would feel a flow of life-force energy of the angel's light entering the top of my head, then pass down my face. I would feel an energy popping sensation inside my face or my sinuses. The flow continued to my palms like a soft wind into the patient. Normally they would mention a feeling of warmth or cold or a tingling sensation in the area which needed help the most. Many times, the feeling went from head to toes. Many patients reported a feeling of deep relaxation or peace in their minds. Some people would see a few minutes of different colored spheres of light or orbs. Some people started to have a vision of their ancestors who had passed on.

I witnessed amazing and life-changing stories of how angel's light helped many people despite limited personal contact during the busy COVID-19 pandemic. I continued to prescribe modern medications as well, but I was careful to prescribe with the smallest needed dosages.

Angel's light has higher energy frequencies that promote and support our own healing ability at the DNA or cellular level. Its intelligence allows it to travel to parts of the body where it is needed most. Everything around us consists of energy vibrating at different frequencies. All of us are connected by energy, so the angel's light can be passed to the recipient using the intention of the mind and by asking the divine team to help. In certain conditions, the angel's light reduced or eliminated the body's discomfort.

Even the severe pain from shingles can be lessened with angel's light. The healing light allows the mind to relax, to be at peace, and to focus better. My patients gained physical and mental energies after a few minutes of treatment. I would regularly reset energy for all my staff at the clinic since everyone was under a great deal of stress during the COVID-19 pandemic. Angel's light supports the relaxation and elevates the coping strength of minds.

Angel's light helps different people in different ways. The lasting effectiveness varies depending upon the person's health. I know that angel's light has no negative side effects. I continue to learn additional information to gain more understanding about this *healing life force energy, angel's light.*

I have discovered that angel's light has the same vibration/energy as the *love* energy that exudes from the heart. Love can travel through space, time, and distance to bring healing power to every individual in the whole world. The power of love will bring peace and healing to everyone it touches.

Other unusual experiences began happening to me. My mind kept sending me back in time more than a couple thousand years ago to ancient Egypt. I was a woman who sat inside a wooden chariot in the middle of a busy city surrounded by many people. I still felt the warmth of the sun, but I felt peace in my spirit while watching my physical body lying with my arm across my chest at the end of that life's journey. I still put my arms across my chest to embrace my heart and calm my spirit in hectic times. Sometimes, while trying to rest at night, I remember the peaceful time of my own death in my soul's memories. Having my arms across my chest and feeling the rise of my chest with each breath reminds me of my current state of living, but I understand the mortality of my physical body. It reminds me to live and enjoy every moment. It reminds me that I have no power or ability to change my yesterday, and tomorrow is not promised either. I must breathe in the life force energy and vitality given to me at this moment. This always helps me return to my state of balance, peace, and center.

When I wake up from sleep the next day, I feel gratitude for the brand-new day. I am thankful for everything I feel, sense, and for all that I see in my vision. People ask me to pick two or three things I am thankful for. I always say, "I cannot do that. Hundreds of things or more come in my mind equally to be thankful for when I'm awakened from my sleep each day. My mind cannot choose or limit only a few things I'm thankful for." I have gratitude for all that I have and for that is yet to come.

My visions sent me back to past lifetimes. I was with a group of women in a secret meeting at a cathedral somewhere in Europe many years ago. The vision showed the other ladies and me wearing long dresses with a tie at our waists, and long sleeves that appeared light and transparent. My vision showed a very large man dressed in bright blue who walked around to guard our safety.

In another lifetime, I was a married man with two children in Japan. I put my family, including two children, my wife, and parents in a little boat and held a lit lantern. Suddenly an atomic bomb went off. I woke up floating but survived in the water. My heart was filled with the deepest of the deep sadness as I realized that I had lost all my family members. I still felt the tremendous deep scar of pain engraved in my soul's memories. I remember feeling my spirit raising up to fight the pain as I felt the calling to rebuild life again from the ashes and the destruction of the war. Somehow this scar on my soul's memory strengthened me through my journey as an old soul.

I would travel back in time in my dreams, probably reliving the experiences embedded within my soul's memories back to places that I may have visited or connected to in past lives. Those places are unfamiliar currently, and I had never heard about them or been there in this lifetime. But later I have found information or pictures that matched my vision on Google or on TV. During one of the experiences, I spent several hours in the evening having conversation and dinner in a mansion. I was sitting at a very long dining table witha man with a distinctive mustache. I interacted with several of his family members including his wife, who was wearing a long dress. I also toured his home and met his horses and his horse keepers. I found out later from watching a television travel program and from personally visiting the Biltmore Estate when I moved to North Carolina in 1998 that I had met George Washington Vanderbilt II, his wife, and his family while recalling or reliving my soul's memories. I had toured his mansion as it was back then. Biltmore Estate is a historic house and tourist attraction in Asheville, North Carolina. It was built for George Washington Vanderbilt II in the late 1800s and is the largest house in the US.

In another dream experience, I visited a place that felt very familiar. I walked around the mountains and stood in front of three stone doors that appeared to be carved into the stone mountain. I drew the picture when I woke up and later found the same dreamed picture on Google. It was the vision of the monumental Tombs of the Kings of Pontus, the masterpiece in

Amasya city of northern Turkey. The tombs were carved into the limestone rocks on Mount Harsena. Per Wikipedia, this impressive archaeological structure belonged to the Kingdom of Pontus and was carved in the limestone rock formation after Mithridates I (who reigned from 281 to 266 BC). The tombs contain large stone grave chambers. This area is called Valley of the Kings.[2] In my dream, the place looked like it was recently created, since all the curved stones were aligned perfectly. The stone mountain in my vision had no trees. The current Google picture shows significant ruins and it is more difficult to see the details. The mountains also appeared to have trees.

I began to have precognitions or future visions in vivid dreams one week before major future events. I saw myself get shot, hit the ground, and then become a bright light a week before a shooting during the Black Lives Matter protests in 2020. I saw myself swept up by a windmill, then thrown into a small boat one week before a hurricane hit in 2020. I dreamed that I was wearing my Air Force uniform and was in a building with many other military members in their uniforms one week before the January 6, 2021, siege on the US Capitol in Washington, D.C. A few days before a high-rise condo building collapsed near Miami, Beach, Florida, in June 2020, I dreamed of many people packed inside an elevator crying out for help. Some people had significant injuries and lost their limbs.

I had some questionable situations in life when I was not sure about the truth or what was hidden. I have heard the repeated whisper in my dreams of the dates that I will be guided to see the truth as it will reveal itself on the date given in my dreams. There were some deceptive situations that I was able to avoid or there were solutions I was guided to discover when the event occurred on the predicted dates.

I used to dream in either Thai or English. Now some of my dreams are in languages that I cannot recognize.

I traveled to another future where there will be houses and buildings that are all tightly connected without any dirt visible between them. There will be dimensions where there are no longer any trees or animals.

People will be dressed in different colored clothes with no visible wrinkles. These people decorated inside their offices and homes with small, manmade green trees. They will tell the story that once upon a time, there were beautiful, magnificent green trees all over earth. Animals, especially dogs, will be robots, and they will be able to sense human emotions. The dogs run as fast as a powerful wind. In my dream, two dogs ran and then sat in front of me after sensing my love for them. People will be wearing metal-like headpieces to protect the personal information in their minds since everyone will have telepathic ability. I went into one shop and tried to choose one headpiece out of many designs.

As an old soul, I was selected again to undergo another challenging life mission. I was sent back to another lifetime on the early morning of Wednesday, November 30, 1966, to experience life challenges that I must conquer before returning to the dimension of light.

PART I

MY FAMILY'S STORY IN THAILAND

My experiences and missions of this lifetime started in 1966.

1

LIVES OF MY ANCESTORS BEFORE I WAS BORN

Many times, we must be shaken our core or knocked to the ground to gain wisdom of life.

Once upon a time in the early 1900s in Chiang Mai, Thailand, a city up north close to the mountains, there was a hardworking, honest family man named Infon. He was my great uncle. He endured many years of hard labor in a liquor factory. He lifted and moved many heavy boxes of liquor with his thin body to earn just enough income for food to care for his family with two children, a boy and a girl. He rode a bicycle every morning to the factory, where he worked from dawn to dusk. The temperature was tropically hot. He hauled things from one building to another. Most of the time, he did not wear a shirt. Sweat soaked his body as he wore old-style traditional northern Thai dark-blue cotton shorts. His shorts were held up at his waist with a long piece of faded of red and white cloth tied in a knot that could be easily released to soak up the sweat that flowed nonstop.

Because of his good heart and a beautiful soul, Infon was chosen by the divine team long before he knew it, but he had to endure the life experiences he needed first. Often we must be shaken to our core or knocked to the ground to gain the wisdom of life needed for the next life's chapters or for important life missions.

One day he experienced the whispering of the light. An angel appeared from the bright light and softly whispered to him, "I am here to be with you. You must prepare yourself and have trust as I step in and become one with your light. You will be the hope, the light, and the healer to your world."

Infon raised his hands in prayers with gratitude and honor and calmly said, "Yes." He felt the coolness and the soft wind of angel's light as his spirit suddenly sparkled brightly with hope, clarity, beauty, and strength. A deep feeling of peace took over the entire space of his mind.

He took a leap of faith. He quit his job and followed the guidance of his angel. He started to wear all white and to do all things with purity in his heart. Every word he spoke had only love, inspiration, encouragement, wisdom, and kindness. He emptied his mind of all worries to fill it with faith and trust. He learned how to quiet his mind from the cares of the world and to concentrate on his breath and his breath only. In the deep silence, he found answers. His spirit was being prepared, for soon he would face and cope with the loss of his best friend, Jai.

Jai was a tomboy kind of girl who grew up with Infon. Ever since they were young, they always hung out together. They played in the rice fields, rode the buffalo together, and were inseparable. They were also together through many of life's tough times. She met an American man who won her heart, and they got married. Sadly, during the honeymoon, she slipped and fell into a deep pond. She could not swim and drowned on her honeymoon. Infon understood through the loss and grief that her light would forever shine, and he knew that soon she would return to earth to meet him again in his lifetime.

The light of her soul came back as a beautiful baby girl who was born to Infon's older sister, my grandmother, Chunpeng. Infon had a total of seven sisters and brothers. The new baby girl was the second child of four who survived out of a total of eleven children.

Chunpeng had lost seven children to childhood illnesses that were mostly preventable or treatable with common medications or treatments. She did not have enough money to seek health care as she herself did not have the resources to see a doctor until her seventies. Unfortunately, by then a significant stroke left her bedridden and with memory loss mostly from undetected long-term high blood pressure. That is why the nickname for high blood pressure, or hypertension, is "a silent killer."

My grandfather got to see a physician for the first time when he visited our family in the US in his eighties. He fell and broke his hip while doing a step exercise on a cement block outside our home. As a physician, I always remind all my patients how important it is to keep up with their health and wellness through prevention. It is a blessing for many people in the US to have some type of health insurance and health-care facilities for getting emergency care without paying up front for services. I know there is still room for improvement in the health-care availability and coverage in the US, but our system surpasses other countries.

My grandmother's beautiful baby girl started to have a high fever and almost went into a coma. She became less responsive during her first week of life. Grandmother again did not seek help from any clinic or hospital since she had no money to pay for treatment. But by this time, Great Uncle Infon had become a healer who had the gift of seeing the soul memories of every human. He recognized this baby's soul from her last life as the life of his best friend Jai.

The angel within him whispered to Infon, "This baby girl

must have a name change to Jai to escape the death list since her soul was just taken recently from earth and her name was already crossed out from the death list." Infon picked up her tiny, limp body and took a few deep breaths. He blew three puffs of air carrying with it the healing light of the angel on the top of her head. Her name then was changed to Jai.

Over the next two days, the new baby Jai began to open her eyes and started to breastfeed normally. She grew up surrounded by nature. Infon would stop by to see her since she was once his best friend from the last life. As she continued to grow, he taught her and reminded her to be brave, to be honest, to work hard, to fill her heart with love, and always to enjoy the little things in life as she had done in her previous life. Uncle Infon always said, *"Heaven is what you create in your heart. Heaven is already where you are and no need to search further. Wherever you go and whatever you do, your angels will forever watch over you."*

Jai was a good child who loved helping with all the household chores. She learned to cook Thai food at a very young age, and she became an awesome chef. My grandparents continued to work hard. My grandmother collected old newspapers that people had thrown away. She folded them by hand, applied glue from boiling potato starch mixed with water, and shaped them into paper bags for sale.

My grandfather would get up daily after being awakened by the morning song of the rooster. He rode a bicycle to work from one side of town to the other. He was a well-known chimney builder. He did not make much money, but he had a high work ethic. He did his best and took pride in laying each brick one by one. He found much joy from the love of creating something to keep people warm in the winter. He worked from sunrise to sunset.

Those chimneys are still standing today to remind the people that once upon a time, there was a skillful chimney master who dedicated his entire life to working with pride. He used the power from his heart to lay each brick one by one perfectly. I learned from my grandfather that no matter what you do, the pride and love that pours from your soul will paint the most magnificent creation on the canvas of life. Your reputation and work will ripple forever through your world.

At this time my Great-Uncle Infon was sharing the angel's light daily from dawn to dusk. People from around the city came to see him. His home was surrounded by people who brought their loved ones who were sick from various illnesses. The outside of his small wooden home looked like a fairground. People put up tents and sold food while they were waiting to see him. There were many people who waited all day to see him for his healing touch.

He was fully guided by his angel to share the healing light. He took time to see each person one by one. He closed his eyes and took a few very deep, noisy breaths. Within a few seconds, he began to speak the voice of his angel. Some of the people came who spoke only Chinese. It was a magical moment to hear the angel in him speaking Chinese back. Yet when Infon was alone without the help from his angel, he did not know any Chinese words and could speak only Chiang Mai (northern Thai) language.

He would gently touch the head of the ones who needed help and blew a few puffs of air to the top of their heads. Suddenly the sick person started to feel better. Some people had psychosis or confusion, but they returned to their normal selves after the healing session. He was called "the healer" or "the medicine man."

When people lost their animals, they asked him to help locate them with his gifted vision. I remember one time it was a buffalo from the rice field. He just closed his eyes for a second and told them where to look for it.

Great Uncle Infon did not speak many words, but each word was filled with comfort and wisdom. He smiled all the time without showing his teeth. People had to watch out because he could travel the world in his mind. He traveled through different dimensions and appeared in people's dreams. He also reminded then that he was in their dreams. He could tell what would happen to people in a minute, a day, a year, and even many years in the future. He would tell people who they were, their names, and where their tombstones were in their last lives.

He said all of us were born with a life destiny. Our roads to get there could be up to us to choose. Once we can figure out our life's purpose or destiny, it is just like locating a compass or finding a key to unlock heaven's door on earth with life's fulfillment and happiness.

2

YOU CANNOT FORCE
A HEART TO LOVE

She decided to escape being a prisoner of life.

Baby Jai was now grown up. She became the most beautiful girl in our village. She had long, thick black hair that flowed and waved with the wind. She walked naturally with grace, confidence, and poise. Her spirit was full of happiness and joy. Her beautiful smile brought love and warmth to the heart of every person she encountered. Everywhere she went, she left the dust of magic as people enjoyed her sweetness. Anyone around her fell in love with her beauty and her cheerful, innocent personality. She also loved to help people and assisted anyone who needed anything done.

With limited income, my grandparents could afford only to let her finish junior high school. But her multiple talents gave her the opportunity to help the community with many events and celebrations. She knew how to sew clothing and cook awesome Thai food. She knew how to create or put together flowers into magnificent flower structures like a parade float. Her talents allowed the town to win many competitions in the flower festivals.

When she turned nineteen, her life took a major turn. A high-ranking officer in the military came to the house and demanded that she be married to him. She knew that her heart could not be forced, and she did not find any love in him. She was deeply sad, and yet she did not lose the tremendous strength she had in her spirit.

She decided to escape being a prisoner of life and left Chiang Mai to go to the big city, Bangkok. Her parents, my grandparents, cried and cried for losing her, but they loved her enough to let her go. She had to fly alone from the nest to find the new place where her heart belonged and to escape from being in a cage forever.

At this point, none of my grandparents' surviving four children were with them. They were in different parts of the country. Their first child, my Aunt Somboon, was a teacher. She was married with two sons, my cousins, Noi and Dang. At that time, Aunt Somboon was divorced and needed my grandparents to help with her two young sons. They stayed with my grandparents. Aunt Somboon mostly stayed at her school in another town.

My grandparent's second child, Uncle Udom, left and joined the military. He was stationed in the Thai Army Base in Bangkok. Their third child was Jai, my mom. Their fourth child was my Aunt Sue, who became a physician and moved to the US in the 1970s.

My mother escaped to be with Uncle Udom and hid herself at the military base in Bangkok. She felt safe and gradually gained enough courage to come out from the base. She found a job at a hair salon near the base and began job training. She was happy to earn an income at her first job. One day as she was leaving work and awaiting a taxi, a handsome young gentleman, an owner of a construction company, stopped his car to speak to her. He asked mom where she was going. She told him innocently that she was headed to a market, but she did not know the direction and she was going alone. She trusted everyone and the world. The young man was concerned for her safety and gave her a ride to the market. He loved her at first sight. He stopped by a few more times at the hair salon after work. After spending more time getting to know Jai, he fell in love with her even more. Her beauty, her honesty, her kindness, her strength, and her innocence had won his heart.

She married him at the age of twenty-two, and this handsome young man named Prasit became my father. They started a family and soon had four living children. They lost one daughter, their second-born child.

3

THE POWER OF LOVE
FROM A MOTHER

Nothing in my soul's journey has had such a beautiful and powerful light as the power of love from my mother.

My mom, Jai, had her first child, my brother Yut, soon after her marriage at the age of twenty-two. He was a happy, easygoing baby who slept well at night and gave mom no problems. Soon after the birth of my brother, another storm of life hit. My father disappeared for one month after losing everything in his business. Mom went everywhere to look for him. Finally, after a month he came home. He had been in jail because of a check that had not cleared. His business partner was dishonest and took all the money in the business account and disappeared.

Mom lost her job as a hairdresser. Both of my parents were jobless with one child. Mom never gave up and fought hard to survive. She started setting up a little shop in front of the apartment. In Thailand, it was common to have street vendors or sidewalk stands to sell things. She made enough money to pay for the apartment and for food.

Life's stresses, her hard work seven days a week, and the loss of my father's job hit like a tornado. Mom then had another baby. My father became hopeless, depressed, and lost. Mom gave birth to her second child and named her Paveena, the same name as mine. Due to the stress, no health care, hard physical work while she was pregnant, and possibly poor nutrition, the baby died at birth. Mom did not find this out until she was getting ready to leave the hospital. The doctor told her that her baby was gone. Her heart broke with crying, but no voice came out, just a river of tears. She dropped to her knees for several minutes in total shock. She gathered all the strength in her soul and put up her hands above her head and prayed, "Please let my daughter come back again. Daughter Paveena, if it is meant to be for you to be my child, come back. Please come back!"

My guidance angel was holding me in the wings of light as my soul slowly floated away from my tiny physical baby body where I was for only nine months in my mom's womb. I listened to her heartbeats, felt her tremendous love, felt the pain of her life stresses, and heard the unspoken worries in her mind.

My spirit started to feel the river of mom's tears that created a burst of light everywhere. I knew that I must return to my mom. I must find a way somehow to come back again to this beautiful soul filled with the tremendous love of a mother. *Nothing in my soul's journey has had such a beautiful and powerful light as the power of love from my mother.*

Somehow, through the matrix of the universe, I found my way back to life. Helped by my guardian angel I came back to earth as her third child. Mom gave me the same name, Paveena, after she had lost me once. I came to the world at a very tough time. There was no place to live and no money to buy food. Mom did not have enough food herself, and her mother's milk ran dry. She could only afford condensed milk. She cried as she feed me condensed milk mixed with water. We soon got kicked out from our apartment. My parents no longer were able to pay rent as the cost of living continued to rise. The guilt of feeding me condensed milk continued to haunt my mom. She apologized to me again when I was already in my fifties. I had to tell mom that she had done her very best to save my life, and nothing is wrong with my physical body from drinking that condensed milk.

My kind Uncle Banyan, dad's cousin, had only a one-room apartment given to him by his work with the Thai government. He felt badly when he saw all of us in such a bad shape. He, with his kind heart and without hesitation, took all of us in. He gave up his little room. He slept the whole time outside the house, on the balcony under a mosquito net, rain or shine.

At this time, mom had another child, Patra. Due to her stress, Patra came prematurely at seven months. She had to be in an incubator. She was blessed and made it out of the hospital after only three days. Mom asked for help to get enough money from family and friends to bring Patra home from the hospital. *Kindness always found us when we needed help.*

Soon came her youngest and last child, Sas. Now with four living children, mom continued to sell food in front of Uncle Banyan's apartment. She cut countless pineapples and sold them. Some days her hands started to bleed due to the high acidity of the pineapple. The people around the neighborhood loved to stop by and buy food to help her. The people loved her for her beautiful voice, her smiles, and her keen memories of people. She would ask about their day, work, family, and situations. She never complained about the difficulties or challenges of her own life. Mom had beautiful smooth skin, and her face glowed and shined like a pearl. The people called her "Maka Nanawn," meaning a beautiful and smoothed-face saleslady.

One day Uncle Banyan's work with the Thai government

changed, and he was ordered to move. The apartment would be demolished, and new construction was scheduled to start. Luckily, my dad's friend offered help and gave us a place to stay. *Again, help from high above always came when we needed it most.*

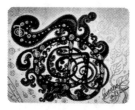

4

I BELONG TO THE FAMILY OF LIFE WARRIORS

The most powerful way to teach the future generations is to live life before them and be there for them.

My maternal great-grandparents worked very hard in the rice fields. I was blessed to spend some time with my great-grandmother before she passed away at the age of ninety-five. My great-grandfather passed away long before I was born. On top of working in the rice field during the season, he also worked in the deep forest finding wood to sell. One day he was very sick and passed away from malaria. As a physician I understand the severity of malaria carried by mosquitoes. I know that untreated cases can progress to severe illness and death within a period of twenty-four hours.

My great-grandparents had eight children who lived near each other beside the family's rice field. They helped in the rice field when they were younger and had more strength. They worked with pride, growing rice to feed the world during many years of their lives. They considered themselves as the warriors of the land. They knew in their hearts that they had created lives for themselves, supported countless human and animals lives with their products, and worked in their own land handed down by our ancestors. They spent most of their lives together in the outdoors where their hearts and spirits were revitalized daily. The healing rays of sunshine, the gentle wind of the rice field, and the songs of the birds kept their spirits bright. The physical labor kept their bodies strong; each had the strength of three men and that was how hard they worked. Children were taught about life, teamwork, honor, respect, love, and world beliefs in the rice field as they took breaks sitting beside their buffaloes.

Unfortunately, I only had a few encounters with my paternal grandparents. I don't know much history of their prior ancestors except that they were Mon people, the first generations in Thailand. They were immigrants from another geographic location south of Myanmar, a kingdom that no longer exists. The war took many Mons lives as the city was destroyed. My grandparents and other family members settled in Pathum Thani, a province of Bangkok. Their stilt homes were situated along or built above the Chao Phaya River shoreline. I remember that they did not have electricity. The only way to get to their houses was via a long narrow walkway made of pieces of wood along the riverside. They collected rainwater in a large clay pot and used it for drinking and cooking. I remember taking baths in the river and using the lantern's warm light for the nighttime.

My paternal grandparents were kind and loving. I met both when they were in their nineties. They spoke only their native language, Mon, which is very different from Thai. I had no idea what they were saying, but their faces showed nothing but love and cheerfulness. I couldn't imagine the strength they had gained in life as they endured the escape from the war during their younger years.

Grandmother had a lot of mangoes on her land near her home. She would make mango rolls when they were ripe from sun drying. She would have a big, happy smile when she handed me those delicious, sweet mango rolls every time I visited. That was the face of kindness I remember. I also never forgot the warm feeling of love from their hearts even though I did not understand the spoken words.

I am so blessed and honored that I belong to the warriors of life. I could not ask for a better soul family to be born into and to begin my life's journey. Having the examples of the people before me and knowing the warrior hearts in them to follow created tremendous inspiration and strength. The best way to live life is by following the examples of my ancestors before me; I have guide rules to follow. The most powerful way to teach the future generations is to live life before them and be there for them. It doesn't matter if life is in the time of outdoor rice fields, the time of no electricity or outdoor bathrooms, or during this modern era. We learn from past generations.

5

THE LONG TRAIN RIDE

I had no concept of past, present, or future. I existed
as a little girl at the beginning of my life's journey.

Mom tried hard to figure out if it was safe for her to return home north to Chiang Mai. Her heart was still in fear because of the reason she had escaped to Bangkok. However, she had no other way out except to return and face the unknown.

Mom had one small bench seat on the train for five people, herself and four children. I remember that long train ride to the new beginning very well. I was born with a photographic memory. I also watched and listened to everything around me. People used to call me a little hawk. I was only three years old. Mom had my brother and sister sitting on the bench-like train seat with her. My youngest sister was a baby on her lap. She laid a piece of an old newspaper she had picked up from a nearby bench and put it on the floor underneath her seat. I was told to stay beneath the seat and sleep on the newspaper.

The train ride from Bangkok felt like an eternity. It took many hours and overnight to get to our destination up north near the mountains of Chiang Mai. I remember listening to the sound of the train and the rhythm of the train track synchronized with the rhythm of the beats of my heart. *I remembered that my brain was like a blank piece of paper with no feeling and no emotion.* I had no understanding of hope, happiness, fear, or dreams. I had no concept of past, present, or future. I existed as a little girl at the beginning of my life's journey.

My dad did not travel with us; he decided to stay in Bangkok with his friend, hoping to find some kind of job.

6

MY SOUL SLIPPED
INTO A DEEP COMA

*Being hopeless as a child with no life training put my
soul in a deep coma.*

Finally, the train reached Chiang Mai. We arrived at our
grandparents' home in a truck with two rows of seats, a kind of
local taxi at that time. Grandfather knew that we were coming.
He had made a little wooden crib from bamboo by hand for my
youngest sister, Sas. She was still a little baby, less than one year
old. I remember seeing her holding onto the rails and halfway
standing up in the bamboo crib watching us. She did not cry.
She did not make any noise, but she looked around with a set of
big bright eyes.

All of us were exhausted, and my mind went blank for many
months after this. *During this time of my life, I cannot recall
anything from my soul memory.* Being hopeless as a child with no
life training put my soul in a deep coma. The light was turned off
in my soul. I could not move. I could not feel. I could not see. I
could not dream. Hope was somehow stuck in a very far distance,
and I could not reach it.

I started to remember again, and my vision of life came back when our dad came from Bangkok to be with us in Chiang Mai since he was not able to find any jobs in Bangkok. Somehow the happiness of seeing him started to rotate the movie like a film of life in my head that had been frozen and on hold for several months. My life started to come into clarity again in my soul's memory.

Unfortunately, and not too long after my dad got to Chiang Mai, I heard my parents having a very loud conversation. It felt like thunder hitting all my inner light. I could not sleep, so I walked over to them and put my little three-year-old body between my mom and my dad. I just looked at them. Both of them told me quickly to go to bed. *It was very dark despite having lights on. The lights were so dimmed in my mind or maybe my spirit had lost hope and my eyes could not see any of the lights.* I stepped out and went to another room, holding on tightly to a door. I sat on a doorstep and tried to fight sleep since something told me bad things were getting ready to happen. That was the last time I saw my dad when I was a little girl.

I had been close to my dad and spent much time with him. He used to carry me on his shoulders. I remember crying myself to sleep every night for several years. The river of my tears kept flowing for thousands of nights.

There was a deep guilt in my heart. For some reason, I blamed myself, thinking that I must have created the fight or that I could not stop the fight from happening between two people dearly loved. *For the first time in my life, I felt responsible for the breakup of my parents.* I stopped smiling. I did not eat much as my love of food and all my hope had left. I remember people started to call me chopsticks since I lost a lot of weight.

Mom also heard the news that the high-ranking officer who had demanded her to marry him died in an accident. There was no longer a reason to fear being back in the city. Crazy things in life happened for a reason. Without this crazy event in my mom's life journey, I may never have gotten the chance to be born to this timeline of life.

7

LET YOUR LIGHT SHINE

*Your soul carries memories from many lifetimes and
with them the wisdom of life.*

My Great-Uncle Infon lived next door to my grandparents. My
grandmother's youngest sister, Great-Aunt CheenJai, also lived
next door. Their two homes were connected, and they kept an eye
on each other. Great-Uncle Infon decided to live his life in solitude
and in silence when both of his children grew up and had their
own families. He continued to work as a healer. With kindness
in their hearts, my Great-Uncle Infon and Great-Aunt CheenJai
frequently called me to spend time with them.

Infon, dressed in all white, sat me down in front of him one
day. He took a few deep breaths. He then touched my head and
blew puffs of air to my head. I started to feel peace in my mind as
the wind of angel's light touched my spirit. He said, "Little one,
don't be sad. This is your life path to learn so your soul can gather
the strength you will need when you grow up." He looked at me
with piercing eyes, deep in thought. He saw the light in me and
understood my future life path and where my soul came from.

The beautiful light in him whispered, *Her training must
start now.*

My great uncle spoke softly. "You were an angel of light and kept coming back to travel this earth. You, yourself, chose to come to learn and explore this earth. You were meant to gain strength through life so that your warrior soul will be awakened to help the people of earth in the future." He asked me to come back to see him daily. He purchased a rotating chair like the ones they use in hair salons. He put my tiny body in it and rotated it gently. He taught me to meditate and silence my mind while the chair rotated in slow motion. He knew that my young mind was distracted and hurt from the chaos of life. He tried to find a way to soothe and calm my spirit. He said, "Let go of the thought of other people in your mind and focus on you and you only. You cannot change anything else except your own thoughts at this moment."

My great-aunt would prepare me all kinds of delicious northern Thai food to fatten me up. I often stayed with her to keep her company. For some reason, I always found myself under the bed every night that I spent there.

Great-Uncle Infon continued teaching me, and I became his young apprentice. He taught me to sit in an Indian-style position, chanting two words, and just two words—"Put tho, Put tho"— while I focused on my breathing.

He said that he heard my mind and asked me why my mind kept thinking and wondering about everyone in my family. He said, "You must silence your mind so you can hear the whisper of your guidance angels and hear your own soul speak. Your soul carries memories from many lifetimes and with them the wisdom of life."

As my great-uncle performed his healing works, I assisted him. His angel would speak to me in a different voice than his and always asked me to accept the invisible healing ball of angel's light. He would drop the invisible ball of angel's light in my mouth, and as I swallowed it I imagined that the healing light went to every part of me to help with healing.

Great-uncle said my heart, my physical body, and my spirit would heal with time. He told me I must heal myself because I had a very important life mission coming in my future. He said, "Just trust, have faith, and believe. You will be guided, and you need no fear in life."

He said, "Never feel alone, because your guardian angels and the spirits of our ancestors are always with you as a team." The most important thing my great uncle said was that he would always be with me even if I could not see him with my human vision.

Even today I continue to feel his presence, and he comes to me in my dreams even though he passed away in the 1990s. Often I smell a particular scent of incense while I'm awake. This makes me smile, knowing that he is visiting me from another dimension.

My sisters and I would stop by to see Great-Uncle Infon. At the beginning, I did not have many friends growing up, but Infon's home was full of friendly spirits. They loved to play. We would play hide-and-seek with all the friendly spirits in his home. They would touch our heads when they found us. Of course, they always found us quickly no matter where we hid. We got used to the friendly spirits and had full trust in them. We did not know or understand that we were fortunate to connect with another dimension of the universe.

With time, my heart gradually began to heal and was awakened to feel the love, kindness, and joy of life again. The light within me that used to appear dimly had regained its brightness. I learned to forgive my little self and with the magic of self-love and self-forgiveness came the full power of hope. I was given a chance to begin another chapter of life. I started to feel like a new butterfly charging into the sun's rays, eager to start another of life's chapters.

My soul returned to my usual curiosity for life, and I looked forward each day for what would come tomorrow.

I started to open up and make friends with all the children in the neighborhood. Most of them were my cousins who were slightly older or younger than I. At the age of five, I began to lead a fun little group of children. We went into the woods looking for tropical fruit. We climbed the fruit trees and had many meals with nature. I no longer had to fight hunger because we could find food everywhere, thanks to our Mother Earth.

One time I was chased by two Doberman dogs. I ran for my life without looking back. I told myself that if I didn't look back and didn't see the dogs, they were not there. I was out of my body as the wind carried me to safety. *Today, I know my little body could not have outrun the two big dogs. Help from above came to save my life again when I needed help.*

Our group would go into the rice fields and look for little fish for my fish tank. Somehow, we managed to get one. I sat on the dirt floor surrounded by my sisters, little cousins, and little neighbor friends and created fun childhood stories in my head to tell them since none of us could afford any books. Their laughter healed my spirit. I finally started to feel that I could make other people heal and be happy with things or stories I created in my mind.

When I was five, my grandparents and my great-aunt taught me how to cook. I became the little chef for my family.

We could not afford an alarm clock, but we never felt that we needed one. *I would wake up with nature's alarm, the rooster crowing. That vibration and the sound of nature awakened my spirit to a brand-new day every morning.*

I helped my grandmother pump water from the ground by hand, build the fire, and then begin cooking or boiling water for the morning bath. Our home would get cold during the winter near the mountains of northern Thailand. Our home was mostly open. We had some wooden walls, but plants made up most of our walls. There were also sturdy dirt floors, shiny from generations stepping on them and sitting on the ground. I even had a few scorpion friends growing up in this home so close to nature.

My Great-Aunt CheenJai next door had a sewing job at her home. I would help her as she taught me how to sew. I remember that my legs were too short to touch the sewing pedal, and I had to halfway stand up to help her work. She treated me well and loved me like her daughter. She would take me on road trips to many places. I got to visit hidden ancient temples, some of them very remote. I got a chance to touch the footprint of Buddha in one of the temples. I also helped take care of her garden, especially watering all the plants and trees. The only water source was a well. I mastered a technique of throwing down a bucket held by a rope into the well. I had to throw the bucket at a perfect angle to pick up enough water. I then carried the bucket of water to the garden. That was my daily physical strength training and exercise.

8

LOVE MUST BE GIVEN, AND A LIFE MUST BE SAVED WHILE LIVING

How can I, as another human being, help others to
pick up the pieces that remain and instill the will to
go on living or to rebuild their life?

My wonderful Great-Aunt CheenJai, who had a beautiful soul of sparkling diamonds, had never been married. She was one of the most beautiful ladies in town, and spoke softly and only with kind words. She never raised her voice at anyone. She was poised and always smiled during conversations, even with strangers. She was very giving despite having little, and she dressed mostly in Thai traditional clothing. She fell deeply in love with a high-ranking officer in the military whom she met at the end of World War II. He was stationed in Chiang Mai, and they dated during that time. He was arranged to be married to someone else when the war ended, and he returned to his home in Bangkok. She had given all her heart and soul to him.

After he left, CheenJai lived life daily in loneliness as her heart and soul had been taken forever by her first love. She never stopped loving him despite knowing that they would never be together. She would wait for his yearly greeting card with a personal message for fifty years until she passed away in her seventies.

She was such a beautiful soul filled with the purest love that ever existed on this earth, yet her love was swept away by the winds of life. She passed away alone in her home. She had taken her beautiful love with her in her soul's memories. Her love was as magnificent as the entire sky, yet was never embraced by earth. Even though more than fifty years have passed, I can still feel the painful essence of her broken heart.

People react to the pain of life with different emotions, strengths, choices, and solutions. At a very young age, I witnessed one of my neighbors hang herself at her own home. The picture of her lifeless body with the rope around her bruised neck hanging from her home's wooden frame remains in the depth of my soul memory. She was an educated and beautiful young woman who suffered from a broken heart after her first love left her for another woman. *The pain from her deep emotional wound had swallowed her whole life as well as the life of her immediate family.*

I remember as a child wondering if I could have done something to help her unlock her spirit from the darkness. I remember seeing her walking around the town slowly with lifeless direction as other children picked on her appearance due to her lack of daily hygiene. How can I, as another human being, help others to pick up the pieces that remain and instill the will to go on living or to rebuild their life? How can I help someone to forget the hurt or transform the hurt into the foundation of the next phase of life? As I am older now, and as a physician, I don't take anyone's sadness for granted. I continue to jump and feel the urgency in my heart that a life must be saved while living.

I have more memories from that time. I started to be very busy helping my grandparents, my great-uncle, and my great-aunt with house chores and other things. I also walked to see another uncle who owned a wood furniture shop. He hired me to sand wood pieces. I earned enough income at the age of four to buy some food, candies, and sweets. I did not see that my income was little. I was grateful for the opportunity to have a job that was important and big enough to keep my supplies of goodies coming.

Life was busy, exciting, and fun. It left no room for any doubts, any self-pity, any negative thoughts, or any feelings of hurt or pain. I look back and see my little self and know that I felt my soul was growing, that my small physical body did not limit me.

Great-Uncle Infon told me, "Always be thankful and focus on what you have, what you see, and what you feel in front of you." *When your life has little, but your spirit has much, you became creative.*

I started making my own toys, including a wooden gun. I used a small, hard berry-like fruit as ammunition. I made a horse from banana leaves, a kite from bamboo and a light piece of paper, and several paper dolls. I had many homemade toys and I was so proud of myself. My heart was full as a child, and I never felt that I lacked anything growing up. The thrill of launching my own homemade kite still glows in my soul's memories. As a child with limitless imagination, I would envision myself soaring with the flying kite as if I were riding a dragon into the blue sky through the clouds.

I grew up fast in my spirit and at the age of five, I started kindergarten. I remember walking across rice fields for thirty minutes to an hour to attend school. Some days the rice fields were so muddy from the rain that it was tough to walk on the foot-wide walkway across the huge field. One day there was a big flood from the nearby Maiping River, and I walked home from school with water up to my chest. I had so much fun because I had never seen so much rain before. I loved running and losing myself in it. My heart did not know enough to be afraid, so I chose to enjoy the moment. As monsoon season continued to hit, I ran and ran under the curtain of the rain, not afraid of the thunder, lighting, flooding, or strong winds. *My heart felt so free, and as a little kid with a big spirit I continued to let it all go.* I let the rain wash away any coming sorrow, and I let the wind blow away any dust of sadness before it even settled on my spirit. I let the tropical sun chase away any darkness before it invaded my light. Whatever I had sitting heavily on my spirit, I just let it all go. I no longer had to compete with the sky to make my own tears. I kept on moving forward as a child of life and never looked back.

9

FACE CHALLENGES WHILE FINDING PEACE AND JOY

I somehow managed to find joy in life without focusing on the obstacles of life that I could not change.

When I started first grade, I got a chance to go to an all-girl school. Then I had to move to another school due to the cost. I was moved to a coed school, Chiang Mai Christian School. At the beginning, it was difficult being new since I had very tanned skin from walking across the rice fields to school every day. Thai culture has skin-tone bias, as wealthy Thais have naturally lighter skin. I was put down as lower class with the term "the rice outside of the rice field." The students also learned that I did not have a father, which became another reason for students to pick on me.

I remember bearing the discomfort of being bullied in school by just walking away. I had to admit that tears came a few times before I began smiling again. I still remember the last time I cried after being bullied at the age of eight or nine. I remember kneeling down on the ground in the middle of the school playground. I saw my own teardrops hit the dirt. I picked up a piece of a tree branch and wrote a promise on the ground that this would be the last time I would cry from being bullied. I told my young self that I was raised in a family of honesty, and nothing I heard was true.

I decided to take control of the "voice traffic" that I would allow to pass into my mind or even deeper into my soul. I remember the teaching from my Great-Uncle Infon that our powerful mind controls our own happiness and our own emotions. No one else has power or access to control our thoughts if we don't let them. I dried my tears and stood up with strength in my spirit that I would stand tall from that moment forward.

Gradually, other students started to like me because I was good with math. I began giving my time helping many of my classmates with their homework or giving them free math tutoring. After a few months, some of the troublemaker kids became my protectors. I was glad that I took care of the situation with forgiveness, love, and peace.

When my youngest sister, Sas, caught up with me at the Chiang Mai Christian School, her classmates bullied her as well. I had walked away when this happened to me, but I could not calm down my protective spirit when this happened to my own family, especially my little sister. I remember walking to my sister's class during my break. I grabbed the neck of the bullying girl. I dragged her out of class. With my strong voice and scary, very dark face, words came from my ten-year-old mouth that I had never said before in my life. I told her that I would be back to kill and bury her if this ever happened again. The girl never returned to the school after that day. Thank God, no one reported me. I would have been kicked out of the school for threatening a younger student.

I grew up with the love for books, especially poetry books, but mom was not able to afford them other than a few schoolbooks. I remember getting up before sunrise and walking half a day to the town's library near the mountain. I did not have money to buy food and would go all day without eating. Luckily, several people were kind enough to put out water in a clay pot in front of their houses with a drinking cup made of a coconut shell. I would stop at those houses to keep myself hydrated under the one-hundred-degree heat of the tropical sun during my long walk to the library. *I would lose myself in the magnificent and joyful feeling of many poetic books.* My soul soared in the clouds with the joy of those beautiful melodies of healing words.

I would return home at sundown. Everyone was too busy with life or with working to notice that I, at age nine or ten, had disappeared most days and on many weekends. *I never allowed a mentality or scarcity or fearful mindset creep into my soul memory as a child.*

I somehow managed to find joy in life without focusing on the obstacles I could not change. I managed to enjoy my long walk. Sometimes I would stop at the waterfall near the mountain to energize my soul and breathe in its beauty. After the mist of the waterfall cooled me from the tropical sun, I would spend the rest of the afternoon at the library. One time as I walked past the zoo a sweet family paid for my ticket to get in. I was able to observe all the animals before making my way to the library.

Mom always said, "If I can bring all the stars in the sky to you, I will do it." In my heart, I always believed this. It makes me grateful for the abundance and lack of limitations in my life.

10

MY SUPERHERO MOM

You must learn to get up and let nobody step on your limbs or your spirit.

My mom turned our grandparent's home into a little grocery shop. She would wake up in the morning before sunrise and head to the big market. She would bring back vegetables, individually packed food, and fruit to sell within our neighborhood. I would wake up with the rooster and go to the market before going to school many mornings to help her carry things. Mom, with her beautiful heart, did not make much profit. She would give away food for free to our family and friends who had limited income.

My Aunt Sue, who had graduated from medical school, was able to help all of us. She bought our grandparents a bigger new home across the street from us. Then we did not have to sleep in the same bedroom with mom. My brother, my two sisters, and I shared a room. We got a three-inch-thick, cotton-filled cushion on the floor to soften our backs and had a mosquito net on top of it. We never noticed the heat despite never having air conditioning in the tropical climate.

My mom was so creative and talented. She expanded her shop downstairs. She made a grocery store in the center area of the first floor. On the right side, she set up two chairs and two mirrors as a hair salon. On the left side, she set up an antique-looking sewing machine. In the back area, she laid out her equipment to make beautiful silk flowers by hand to sell.

At night my superhero mom was a taxi driver. I could not sleep many nights worrying about her. I would sit on top of the stairway and wait for her to return home, usually after midnight. She knew that I would wait for her. She always stopped and got my favorite treat—roti, a round flatbread native to India that was cooked on a griddle. She also sold life insurance and health insurance during the daytime. Her work ethic and strength were unmatched by anyone I have ever encountered in my entire human life. As she frequently said to me, "My daughter, you are not a tree. If life ever takes you down to the ground, you better get up. The tree limbs will break and be stepped on by humans after its fall. You are unlike a tree. You must learn to get up and let nobody step on your limbs or your spirit."

I moved forward in school and my mom was able to afford my last year of junior high school. I loved my school so much, and I loved everyone in my class. I became one of the class officers and the student counselor. My tough experiences as a child became my biggest strength in helping others. I spent my lunchtime and after school tutoring my classmates who needed help. I spent countless hours counseling my classmates who had gone through life's tough situations, including the loss of their loved ones. Somehow my little heart could feel their pain, since I, too, had overcome similar pain. The feeling of it is imbedded in my soul's memories.

I was meant to learn the toughest lessons of life at a very young age since I was destined to help others. I would get up early every morning during my walk to school. I stopped at a bakery to pick up a tray of chocolate cake. I earned some money by selling them in school in the morning before my classes. I was able to save up enough money to buy the whole class Christmas gifts and goodies at the end of the year. *I started to feel that my purpose in life must be bigger than just myself.*

I continued to listen and help others cope with their life's crises as if it were my calling or my duty as a person.

I never missed any days of school despite being sick with a cold or a fever, knowing that each day of school was equal to my mom's sleepless nights from her hard work. School in Thailand was not free. People had to pay for everything, including tuition, books, and uniforms. *If students could attend school, they were beyond blessed.*

Eventually mom was able to make enough income to hire a tricycle service that gave us rides to our school. Mom was so proud of us. I remember her biggest smile every time she got a chance to visit our school. I was able to graduate in 1981 from junior high school and received the highest award given to a single student each year. The plaque was made from real silver and engraved with "The Best Student of the Year." My dream used to be so simple. I dreamed that one day I would get a chance to go to high school. High school was very expensive, and students had to test and compete with the students in the whole city since schools were so limited in Thailand. *Looking back now, I am glad that I started with the one dream of finishing high school.* I always kept on dreaming because my soul refused to quit. Every dream I had might seem big or small to other people, but nothing else was as magnificent for me. Every dream that I was able to achieve became the foundation of the next dreams, and collectively, they became who I am as a woman in today's lifetime.

This same year, my oldest brother, Yut, also graduated from an all-male school with the best all-around award for his 4.0 perfect GPA on top of playing every sport. He was also in every musical band. Yut is an amazing warrior soul. He was on the school football (soccer) team and basketball team. He was in the regular school band and the traditional Thai musical band. His school life was very busy, and I hardly remember being around him much. Although we shared little time, he always was my childhood role model. He always said, "Just do it. You can do it, and you have all the strength you need to do it." He frequently told me, "Anything you ever need from me, I will always help you. No worries. If I have to throw myself in front of the train to save you, I will do it." His brain was like a computer. He had answers for everything in the world. He always excelled in whatever he did, and later he graduated at the top of his medical school class.

When we were not in school, we played in nature. We had a bodyguard named Rummy. He was a very smart dog who was sent to earth to protect us. Dang, my cousin, named Rummy because he appeared while Dang was playing a card game called rummy. We love playing hide-and-seek with this dog. This big black dog protected us from anyone who came around us with negative energy. Believe it or not, this dog could see through souls and smell any bad intentions toward us. He never needed any leash as he knew his life purpose as our keeper. He never left our sides and never gave up on us no matter how many times we had accidently stepped on him or pulled his tail. He taught us humans to love unconditionally, and that love comes with forgiveness.

11

DANGER WAS IN FRONT OF ME

Life is meant to be happy, to be joyful, to be loved.
You are meant to experience good health, to encounter
loving relationships, and to experience all the beauty
of life and the beauty of the world.

Our home continued to grow, with more relatives living with us—my Grandmother Chunpeng; my Grandfather Chuntip; my mom, Jai, who by this time had married my stepdad, Insorn; my two cousins, Dang and Noi; my brother Yut; my sister Patra; my youngest sister, Sas; and me.

My mom's oldest sister, Somboon (mother of Dang and Noi), also came back home to live with us after being diagnosed with metastatic cervical cancer. She had to have surgery that removed not only her uterus and ovaries but parts of her colon. She had a colostomy and a bag on the side of her abdomen. A home health nurse came by to check on her. The nurse taught me how to care for Aunt Somboon and her colostomy bag. I promised Aunt Somboon before she passed away that I would become a nurse. *Here again, my dream list was added to, or promoted by, another life's challenge or situation.*

I remember very well the day that she passed away. I was sitting

43

in a class, and suddenly my tears started flowing for no reason. I knew in my heart that I would no longer see her. I hurried home after school, and more tears came as I saw her lifeless body after she left this earth. Her soul had completed her life journey, but I was not sure if she had completed her life's mission.

That was more than forty years ago, and I still speak to her from my heart. I continue to speak to her spirit and let her know that I kept my promise of being a nurse. I kept on dreaming and finished medical school as well.

My cousin Dang was a very hard-working man who was older than me. He had a dream that one day he would open the best noodle shop in the city. Soon after he mentioned it to me, he opened a very cool noodle place. He had created a unique noodle recipe. I remember how delicious it was. He soon became the owner of a noodle shop that is now well known in Chiang Mai. Many movie stars and people in politics, including the former prime minister of Thailand, came to his noodle shop. *He showed us that if we dreamed it and acted from our hearts and souls, it would happen.*

Unfortunately, he did not live long enough to see the continued success of his noodle shop. He passed away in his sleep due to an unknown cause at a young age. At that time, he was married and had two sons. His wife was a hard-working lady named Samerjai. She smiled often and was kind to all of us. One of his two sons had a motorcycle accident and passed away at the scene of the accident when his chest was punctured by the motorcycle handle. His remaining son, Thermsak, married and had one sweet daughter, Deam, who now calls me grandma.

Sadly, my other cousin, Noi, got in very deep with the wrong group of people. He started to do heavy drugs and brought some friends to our grandparents' home. No matter what happened or the wrong road he took, he loved all of us like his own brothers and sisters. He always wanted to protect us. He did not want us to be like him. I remember going into the bag he kept hidden behind a shelf near the bathroom and throwing away all the drugs he had.

I cannot not erase this picture of one night from my mind after many years in my soul's memory. I came down to the lower level late at night to use the bathroom. When I came out of the bathroom, I stood face-to-face with a man in the dark. He was only one foot in front of me. Something in my spirit and soul told me that I was in a grave danger. I thought, *I had better prepare to fight for my life.* A voice behind me was very loud calling my name. The strong voice of my grandmother saved my life. The intruder ran off. My team of angels had awakened my grandmother from her sleep to come downstairs and save me. *I believe that having faith and trust will always help me when needed. Thank you, my divine team and the spirits of all my ancestors, who continue to protect me throughout my life's journey.*

I continued to worry so much about Noi. I spoke to him as a child with a spirit that was filled with truths. I remember telling him to stop seeing or being with all the people that made him not be himself. I knew inside my heart that my cousin Noi had a beautiful soul. His light was beautiful, but drugs had covered all his light. He was put in jail for many years. I tried to locate him and visit him at different jails since he often moved from one to another. I continued to write letters to him from the US after we left Thailand. Many years later, I received the news that Noi had died from a drug overdose when he was finally released from jail many years later. I still talk to his light and hope that he will return to earth one day with a better experience. *Life is meant to be happy, to be joyful, to be loved. You are meant to experience good health, to encounter loving relationships, and to experience all the beauty of life and the beauty of the world.*

PART II

LIFE IN THE UNITED STATES OF AMERICA

12

THE JOURNEY ACROSS
THE WORLD

*Maybe staying curious about life had kept my spirit
from breaking down.*

My mom's youngest sister, Aunt Sue, who is the pioneer of our
family, got an opportunity to travel to the United States to begin
her residency training in family medicine. She subsequently
worked as a family physician. Aunt Sue started a process to bring
mom to the US.

By this time, mom had met my stepfather, Insorn, and they
got married quietly, just the two of them. He came to live with
us and our grandparents. Mom called him Uncle Insorn for fear
that we would not accept him. After all these years, I still call my
stepdad "Uncle Insorn."

Uncle Udom's family, including his four children, my mom,
and my stepdad, were supposed to relocate from Thailand to the
US first. My brother, two sisters, and I were supposed to wait a
few more years. My heart was sad and broken learning that my
mom would be leaving all four of us with our grandparents.

I went to my Great-Uncle Infon's home and was very
distressed. He came out and said I should no longer worry. We

began packing, as his vision of the future told him something different from what we thought was going to happen. He said, "You will be going to the United States with your mother and stepfather." Within a few weeks, we received word from Aunt Sue to start packing. All four of us would be traveling to the US together with our mom and stepfather.

It did not take me much time to pack since I only had three or four outfits and one pair of shoes. Sometimes having a simple life is a blessing. I did not have to let go of many things. *People can be emotionally connected to their belongings. Their minds will not rest or be at peace until they carry all their possessions when traveling across the world.*

I had mixed feelings and fear of the unknown when thinking about moving halfway across the world to another country. I was happy to travel together with my mom and my family, yet my Thai spirit felt the longing to be in the ancient land of Siam. I knew that I would greatly miss other family members and friends I had grown up with.

Not only would I be missing all my family and friends, but I would miss myself and the person that I was while I lived my life in Thailand. It was very hard for my heart to say goodbye, knowing there was a possibility I would not be able to return to Thailand in the future.

I made time to visit and say goodbye to all my family and friends in Thailand as well as the spirit of the land that had protected me while I walked this beautiful Mother Earth. I grew up with a habit of asking permission and protection from the spirit of the land everywhere I go.

Every family member, including my Great-Uncle Infon, came to bid us farewell at the train station. We began our longest journey by an overnight train traveling from Northern Thailand to the capital city, Bangkok. We then caught the flight to Korea, then flights to Alaska and to West Virginia.

My heart was pounding as the train pulled out of the station and I saw everyone get farther and farther away. I can still see the smile of my Great Uncle Infon as his vision of the future told him that I would be back soon to see him again. Once again, on this second important train ride to a new beginning in my life, the rhythm and the sound of the train track synchronized with the rhythm of my heartbeats.

We arrived in Bangkok and were able to sleep on the floor of a relative's home while waiting for a flight to the US. I remember sleeping on the hard floor with no pillow, with nothing else in my mind except getting ready for a new life chapter in a new far away land.

I never stopped being curious about life, and I kept asking myself what my next chapter would be like. Maybe staying curious about life had kept my spirit from breaking down.

I was able to see my own father at the airport since we had recently reconnected before the trip out of Thailand. He was remarried and had two sons, Tom and A. I got to say goodbye to him while he voiced his disapproval of our decision to leave the country. We had to give up my dad's last name and change it to my stepdad's last name to be able to go through the process of traveling as one family. I was all grown up then at the age of fourteen, and the distance between our hearts grew like an ocean between our souls. I remember being happy for him that he had a new family and was no longer alone.

My tears never stopped flowing throughout the many days of the trip across the continents. The excitement of the new life could not calm me or bring me enough courage to stop the crying of my little soul that was vibrating in confusion.

Our flight took us halfway across the world safely to the land we could only imagine in a dream or see from a few pictures in our schoolbooks.

The long trip felt like an eternity. We finally landed in "Almost Heaven," West Virginia, in July 1981. The mountains reminded me of my home in northern Thailand. The green trees refreshed my first vision of this new world, and this vision continues to be imprinted in my soul's memories as the beginning of life in the United States.

13

KEEPING MY PROMISE

Every spoken word holds the magic of life and death.

My aunt's medical clinic had a small area with built-in quarters in the back, and we stayed there during the daytime. At night we slept on the floor in the empty exam rooms at her clinic. Soon afterward, more bedrooms were added to the back of her clinic. I was blessed to have a room that I shared with my two sisters and two more girls, my cousins.

We did not need much closet space, since we only had a few things until we received some donated clothes from my aunt's friends. Mom also sewed us a few more outfits. We used to wear uniforms to school in Thailand. Learning that we could wear anything to school in the US made it easier.

I started high school soon after we arrived in West Virginia in 1981. I attended Herbert Hoover High School in Clendenin. My mother was able to work as an assistant in my aunt's medical office. She was happy to work only one job. I also was surprised and almost cried when I saw a school bus drive right up in front of my home to pick us up. I no longer had to walk across the rice fields in the tropical heat, the rain, or storms to school. I cannot express how grateful I was that I was given free books and free schooling while I attended high school. I got a little choked up on my first day walking to the bus.

My heart was pounding because I had never seen so many Americans on one bus. I could not understand any of their conversations. *I pulled out my survival face and smiled.* Maybe this is when my forever smiling face began. I tried my best to develop a friendly version of myself as I could not verbally express much in English. Even today, I still smile a lot.

We used to eat rice with all of our meals, and it was my first time eating bread for breakfast. Bread was just too expensive, and it was a treat if we were able to find it in Thailand. It was so delicious that I ate about ten pieces of bread with peanut butter from a big gallon container.

Soon my aunt bought a two-level home about fifteen minutes from her clinic. I was able to stay in a bedroom with just my two sisters, which was a great improvement.

Since I was the oldest girl, I became the chef for the house and did all the cleaning and laundry for everyone. My evenings were long since I could not finish all my daily house chores until after dark.

My ability to read and write English was very limited back then. Every night I went to a quiet closet with books from my school, an English-Thai dictionary, and a glass of cold water to wet my eyes when I got tired. I patiently translated all my books word for word from English to Thai before all my classes. Knowing that I had a high school to attend was my biggest dream came true. This gave me much strength and motivation to do everything needed to succeed. I felt like I was one in a million.

I am so grateful for the little things in life that seemed so big to me. My heart was blessed to live in this country with advanced technology. Everything is simple and convenient. Many people may not even see the importance of these ordinary things.

Turning on the faucet and seeing clear drinking water coming out and using as much as I like is beyond a blessing. At times, it brought tears to my eyes. Growing up in Thailand, I had to hand pump water from the ground little by little. I spent a long time building the fire to boil the water or warm it to use for a bath on cold mornings. I had to run the water through a homemade filter system made of multiple layers of sand and stones in a large clay pot before I could drink it or use it for cooking. Washing clothes by hand took me two days.

I hope more people realize that many little things are not so little for many people in other parts of the world. When you appreciate every small detail in life, you will feel very fortunate, and your soul will sing constantly with joy. For this reason, I must tell everyone in the US that each of you is truly one in a million.

I was blessed to go to a high school with friendly and kind students and teachers. I remembered that my classmates were trying very hard to teach me how to speak English a few words at a time. Some of the cool slang words were not in the dictionary, like "howdy" for hello!

I remember my English teacher, Sharon Paxton, very well. She will forever have a space within my heart. Because of her dedication and her amazing human soul, she took extra time on the weekends to come to our house and teach all of us how to speak and write English. If all the teachers in this world had as much love and compassion as she has, the whole world would be filled with successful future generations. I continue to tell all the teachers I encounter in life that teachers have a special space in my heart. My ability to read or write English helps me with everything I do. It has been the key for my success in every chapter of my life's journey.

Without communication skills, we will not last as human beings. Every spoken word holds the magic of life and death. Words can ignite life, love, joy, inspiration, courage, and happiness in the hearts of people, and at the same time, words can strengthen or break down the life of a soul. Every word that comes from our hearts and souls is imprinted with the beautiful energy of love and the dark energy of hate. We must pause and give thought to our words before they escape the door of our being. The key that unlocks the power of every word is the intention from our powerful minds. Everything runs in orbits or cycles. Every positive intention or negative intention in every word of mankind will circle back into our own energy space and strike our souls with the same effects and magnitudes.

I love to draw, and I began drawing portraits on the weekend for extra income. I also was honored to draw a huge picture of space shuttle Challenger charging forward into the deep blue sky on one wall of our science class. I had a deep connection in my heart with the space shuttle after studying it and drawing it. Looking back again during my college years, I remember watching the news on the television while standing at the cafeteria. My heart shook so badly while watching the Challenger disaster on January 28, 1986, when it exploded and killed all seven crew members.

I tried sports in high school for the very first time. We had no way of paying for any toys or sports equipment when we were in Thailand. I started to play tennis for my high school tennis team and learned how to play table tennis. I love table tennis so much that I spent as much time as I could practicing during my lunch break in school. I was pretty good at table tennis in a short time. Several students and my gym coach, Coach Kee, loved to challenge me to play. I also made time to practice tennis on some evenings and weekends.

My first strange food was pizza. It amazed me how the long strands of mozzarella cheese would stretch when I tried to eat them. I know now, of course, that pizza is not a traditional

American food. Fast food was unheard of in Thailand in the 1980s. Now Thailand has many fast-food restaurants, including McDonalds—whose foods is actually considered to be fancier and more expensive than local Thai foods. I remember feeling very happy eating chocolate and raisins. These simple treats are common in the US but expensive in Thailand.

My family was somewhat strict, and I was not allowed to hang out with any friends outside of high school or talk to them on the phone. I would not have had any extra time anyway with all the house chores that I was responsible for. I was not allowed to date at that young age. I remember going to prom alone, but I enjoyed my time there with all my friends. I was wearing a long pink dress with high neck and long sleeves. I got a chance to dance a few songs borrowing some of my friends' prom dates.

Our word is our soul's honor. We are what we do and not what we say we will do. I never forgot my promise to my Aunt Somboon, who passed away with cancer, that I would one day become a nurse.

I was also given free schooling at Carver Career Center for nursing assistant training. I continually tell children in the US that they must be grateful for being born in a country that loves children and has the economic power to support its citizens with free schooling to the twelfth grade.

I signed up for and attended the nursing assistant school at Carver Career Center during my last year of high school. Our class got a chance to train at the local hospital and nursing homes. I learned many medical terms, how to draw blood, how to make hospital beds, how to turn patients or use a patient lift, and how to help patients with activities of daily living including bathing and bedpan use. I fulfilled my childhood dream of finishing high school as well as beginning the journey to keep my promise to my Aunt Somboon. I graduated with honors from both high school and nursing assistant career training in 1984. I received funding from winning a contest to buy equipment to support my training at the Carver Career Center. I remember my mom's big smile at my graduation as her second child was on the way to college.

By this time my older brother had already started premedical school at West Virginia University. He had graduated from high school with honors as well. He won a scholarship, but also had a student loan and work study to pay for college, since mom's income was not enough to support us. We had no expectation for mom to help us with college. *We asked about, looked for, searched, and studied every possible way to fund our own college educations. We had faith and trusted in our heart that college would happen, and it did.*

Years later, in 2016, we learned that our Herbert Hoover High School buildings were severely damaged by flooding. Water from nearby Elk River had swallowed our high school without mercy. Seven to ten feet of water had caused significant damage beyond repair. Our fond memories as our place of the new beginning in the US has never left our hearts and souls even though the physical building was demolished and is no longer standing.

Despite the craziness of Facebook, I am so grateful that it allows me to stay connected with several of my high school classmates and teachers and to my family and friends in Thailand. Life and time keep moving forward without a break. Many of my classmates have become parents and grandparents. I have also lost some friends and family members during the more than forty years of my life's journey since I stepped foot on US soil.

14

TIME TO LEARN
COMPASSION AND *LOVE*

When a life story is calling us to be in it, we will get
pulled into this theater of life by some kind of strong
force that our soul cannot resist or understand.

After graduating high school, I applied to nursing school and was
accepted into West Virginia University. I had no money and no
help for schooling. *I kept on believing and never lost my hope and*
faith. I know in my heart that help will always appear when needed.

I showed up at the college's financial assistance office asking
for help. I applied for work study, student aid, and scholarships
and was lucky to get help from all three. I worked in the school
photo developing room and library while going to college to earn
extra income for expenses.

I was destined to learn what it was like to be a sick person
before I could be a health-care provider for other people. At the
end of my first year in college, I became very sick overnight.
A black cloud of smoke suddenly appeared in my vision in the
ceiling of my bedroom. That dark cloud somewhat frightened
me. It dropped down on top of my body before engulfing me,
and I could not move or breathe. The sickness appeared as smoke

from a demon in my vision. I remember falling asleep as if I were hypnotized. I woke up in pain and was unable to walk the next morning. Every joint in my body was swollen, red, and locked. I could not get up from the bed until the next day.

I was able to find help and went to the student health clinic for an evaluation. They ran many blood tests that showed that my inflammation levels were significantly elevated. The test for lupus showed elevated levels. Of course, I did not tell my doctor about seeing the black cloud the night before I got very sick. Because of my limited English, the doctor had to call my aunt, Dr. Sue. He wanted me to see a rheumatologist as quickly as possible.

The rheumatologist told me that I had to take myself out of college, stop playing all my sports, and start the treatment for lupus. He said that I would not be able to handle any more stress from life or physical stress to my body. He said that I would not survive without the recommended medications because the illness would affect many of my organs.

Well, guess what happened. I was a hardheaded teenager with an old soul and the strong belief that I would rather die than not keep my promise. I had been given a chance in life to go beyond my original dream of finishing high school. I decided that I would not throw this one chance away. I also knew in my heart that I had to fulfill the promise to my dying aunt to become a nurse. I refused to quit college and I did not show up for my rheumatology follow up appointment or treatment. I told my family that I would rather die in college doing things I was dreaming of than to quit my life's journey.

As I look back now, I know that I had to go through this serious setback of my health for a bigger reason. My soul's memory gained compassion toward every sick person I have encountered in my career as a nurse and a physician.

I was truly blessed and lucky to recover from this illness

without any medical treatments, but I do not advise anyone to not get help when they are sick.

At the time of my illness, I was involved in helping new international students to transition or adapt to student life in the US. I also became the president of Thai Students in America at my college. A group of international students I met began take turns in helping me with cooking and bringing me things that I needed. *Help comes again when it is needed the most.*

I also found a piece of an old paper given to me by my Great-Uncle Infon before I left Thailand. He knew that someday, I would need a magic mantra to bring the power of self-healing into focus. The paragraph was written in an old Sanskrit language. When I was very little, he taught me to read before meditation. I started to read and meditate daily focusing my mind only on self-healing.

I gradually got better on my own after a couple of weeks. I went back to have my inflammation levels retested, and the tests came back normal. I soon resumed all my normal activities and sports with no limitations or discomfort. *My life went back to being normal, and I put another soul experience behind me in the depth of my soul memories.* This experience was hidden deep from my mind, so it no longer put any limitations in my future life journey.

I also learned that stress could worsen lupus or any illness. *I started to instill mind awareness.* I was in a hurry to feel better, so I learned quickly to empty junk from my mind. This left it emptier for positive thoughts.

Being told as a young person that you will die from an illness had put a new perspective in my early vision on life. It pushed me to hurry and live the predicted short life I may have left on another level and to seek harder for joy.

I became aware that stress can destroy life. I also discovered that peace from within would be healing medicine. I gave myself permission not to worry so much and not to allow others' negative talk inside my mind. I told myself that it is okay not to be stressed all the time. Of course, it is a constant fight to stay destressed in a world full of stresses and negativities. It is still helpful to consciously put my mind into absolute alertness to fight stress or to block as much stress as possible. It is like placing a double door as a gate to my own mind. *We are with ourselves the most, so we need to talk to ourselves nicely.* We live life in at least two dimensions, in our mind and our physical world. The energy of the two dimensions vibrates together. When our mind lives a healthy and joyful life, our physical life will be more healthy and joyful as well. It is important that we treat our mind as a treasure box for beautiful, creative, inspiring, and healing thoughts. Many of our worries are not necessary or are out of our control. Our mind is creative and has an ability to create worried thoughts that may not even exist in the real physical world. We must find a way to stop or control the production of this defective and harmful thinking. It is important that we choose to live a beautiful life and love story, for one day each of us will become a memory in someone's thoughts.

It is important to realize that we need to create a conflict-free environment to house our light in the world to be free of conflict and stresses. There is a space within us that we can keep conflict-free by removing any negative thoughts and negative energy from it during our entire life. This is the space that we can fully control. *Once our space is free from conflict, we can better hear our soul and our divine team speak. This flow of communication from our higher source will bring more harmony to our lives. We will become the best version of ourselves, with unstoppable creative ability. We will feel more peaceful everywhere we go in the world because we take this conflict-free home of light with us.*

In today's world there is a free flow of information. We

are blessed with advanced technology, but we must use it with great caution. We must have balance and be very selective about the information we choose to read or accept. All information carries energy that can affect our own beautiful inner light. I feel heaviness in my energy field with certain TV programs or certain movies. *I may listen enough to keep up with the world, but I pull back when needed to protect my energy field. We must be selective in what information we allow into our lives and our minds.*

I earned enough income in the work-study program in college to afford an airplane ticket back to Thailand to visit all my family and friends during my second year of college. I was happy to see them again. My Great-Uncle Infon blew angel's light on my head. My heart was happy, and I knew that I would again return for another visit. The distance across the world would never forever separate me from the people that I love in my birth country.

Infon warned me of an upcoming life challenge that my heart would have to experience. He told me that my first love would be my painful lesson, and that I would meet my husband after this lesson. Infon predicted that I would meet my husband and bring him back to see him in 1991.

Even today, it is hard for me to reason how our life's path and story had already been destined or written within the book of life. Would I be able to skip or even think about skipping a life chapter to avoid heartaches and pain? I don't think so. *When a life story is calling us to be in it, we will get pulled into this theater of life by some kind of strong force that our soul cannot resist or understand.*

During my second year of college, in 1985, I met Abby, a sweet and handsome boy from India who came as an international student to study mechanical engineering. I started dating for the very first time in my life and fell in love for the very first time. I was Abby's first love too, or so he told me. We started planning and talking about getting married after almost three years of dating.

His parents came from India when both of us were graduating from college. I was graduating with a bachelor of science degree in nursing, and Abby was graduating with a master's degree in mechanical engineering. I remember how excited my heart was to finally get a chance to meet his parents. I was deeply disappointed and very heartbroken after learning that Abby was arranged to be married when he got back to India. Abby refused to let me meet his parents, and he had never told them about me. I totally forgot the prediction from my great-uncle, as love had blinded me to everything. I was destined to learn the pain of heartbreak.

My life path was meant for my soul to learn from more storms of life, and my young spirit was put to another test. It was just the beginning of my life lessons in love. I could not understand at that time how something as pure and beautiful as love could turn my heart into dust in the wind within a second.

The experience brought me such deep disappointment that no words were enough to express or comfort the pain. There were just no pieces of my heart left to be put back together. I remember that my young spirit and my zest for life suddenly left me as if a quickly spinning tornado had taken a spin in the center of my whole existence.

When you love with all your innocent heart and soul there was no room left for the unexpected crashing down of what happens in life. Learning to let go of what I thought was a real, true love was the hardest lesson. It was also hard to tell myself that I could not reject myself when someone or some life situation had rejected me. It was hard to realize that love of self comes first and I should not let my heart depend on the world around me to feel love.

I remember driving across a bridge in the darkness of night and stepping on the gas pedal as hard as my right foot could. *My team of angels saved me.* I felt the bright light suddenly strike in the middle of my mind and awaken me from the smoke of sadness. *This was the whisper of the light moment in my subconscious when I must be awakened from the pain.* It was the vision of my mom and all the sacrifices she had to make to raise me up to this point. My foot lightened its force on the gas pedal as I decided that my own life was worth living.

Sometimes our soul gives up and just wants to sit and burn when we see the fire of life in front of us. *We don't know that we simply need to turn around to see the clear path to live life another day.* Sometimes we don't realize that the tornado of life comes to disrupt and clear our paths for other, better chapters of life that need to begin.

I learned as I grew older that true love never breaks anyone's heart. Once your heart gets wounded, it gains strength and becomes unbreakable. Once you heal, the dust in the wind will uncover the bright diamond buried deep beneath that had always been there. Your heart forever shines bright and carries with it tremendous strength to rise and love again. Most important of all is learning to love yourself and knowing that you are the one all along who forever carries the vessel of unconditional self-love.

I looked back many years later with forgiveness. My heart felt pain for Abby, who had to follow his family's traditions and culture. I still believe today that he did not have a choice because of his family tradition, but he could not stop his heart from loving me. This choice was not available to him because his culture. I continue to send positive wishes across the continent for him to be happy in life.

I learned later that Abby had been so heartbroken he refused to return to India. He was searching for me. I finally made a phone call and spoke to him. I had to tell him the hard truth that I would not return to continue life with him. He needed to go on living life. Many years later, I found out that he had gone back to India, got married, and had children.

Little did I know then that as a family doctor I would have the occasion to share this story with many teenagers who had gone through similar pain from the heartbreak of love that was *unreal.* I was able to put myself in the soul shoes of my young patients as I listened to their disappointment and pain as they learned about relationships and love.

After finishing nursing school and passing the exam to be a registered nurse, I returned home to Big Chimney, West Virginia, and started working at Saint Francis Hospital in 1988. By this time my brother had entered medical school, and my two sisters began pharmacy school. *I was beyond happy to reach another dream and have the chance to do something that my heart loves—caring for other human beings.*

During my nursing career, I cared for a patient in coma. I continued speaking to him and assured him that he was being cared for to the best of my ability. He finally recovered, woke up from the coma, and told me that my voice had kept him trying to return to his life. It has been many years, and most of that memory has left me except the lesson. *Our hearts must not give up that easily.* Continue to extend love and inspire every soul, no matter the condition of the physical body. We can instill the will to live in the spirit within.

15

NO HURRICANE
COULD STOP ME

*As humans, our life's purpose in any lifetime must
always be bigger than just ourselves.*

In 1988, I met my husband, Tommy. He is also Thai and came
to the US in 1971. He was on the same soccer team as Yut, my
brother. They played friendly soccer games for the Queen Cup
in Washington, DC, for the Thai Association in America. The
contest honored the queen of Thailand.

Tommy kept finding a way to sit beside me at the cheering
bench. He was from West Virginia too and needed a ride back
since he had come to Washington with a friend. The six-hour car
ride back home and our similar culture and background as Thais
enabled us to understand each other quickly. My prior heartbreak
taught me that I would be in a better life situation when I met
someone with many similarities of culture and background. We
both had so much to talk about and were able to share our life
experiences since he had been in the US as an immigrant since
1971. He came at a tougher time than I did, and he had to share
a one-room apartment with five other Thai friends. He mentioned

walking long hours in the snow to work and sleeping in the closet with an old phone book as his pillow.

The day after we got back to West Virginia, Tommy showed up while I was playing tennis with my family. We started dating.

He was working for Blue Cross Blue Shield in the graphics department. That same year my mother and my stepdad had to give up their jobs due to ill health and other life events. I decided to join Cross Country Nursing since the pay was much better and my family needed the assistance. I had to support my family since all my siblings were still in college. Tommy was so kind that he took all my family in. They stayed in his modular home with three small bedrooms. *Again, help came at the right time as needed.*

I was sent to Sumter, South Carolina, as a traveling nurse for my first assignment. I sent all my paychecks home to Tommy to help care for my family. He kept telling me that he would be waiting for me.

Hurricane Hugo hit South Carolina in 1989 and the eye of the storm went through the town. I slept in the closet alone, listening to the radio as the eye of the storm shook the city with a wind speed of 120 miles per hour. My neighbors evacuated the apartment building except for two young men near my apartment. The strong wind was bending all the trees in front of me, and the whole sky was pitch black as I stepped outside to look. The gusts of wind sounded like the earth was being hit by multiple asteroids. That moment I had a dark thought that the day might be my last day on earth. I picked up a landline to call my family and Tommy while it was still working. I told them not to worry about me, but my heart was actually saying goodbye.

I witnessed devastating conditions in the morning. There was damage to many buildings and no running water or electricity. The phone was no longer working. I took a shower outside in the storm that early morning before the sun rose, and drove my car to work across many fallen trees and power lines. There was no time off or calling in sick. I told myself that sick patients needed me to be there. *As humans, our life's purpose in any lifetime must always be bigger than just ourselves.*

The hospital was dark and had only a few dimmed emergency lights. Not many staff members were there. Another nursing assistant and I were running back and forth between two hospital wings. There was no running water. We used baby wipes to care for our patients. We could not respond to all the needs or check on everyone often enough. I couldn't contact doctors when I needed their help. I remember one elderly man passed away before I got to him. All I had time to do was to say farewell to his spirit and apologize for not being there for him at his last breath on earth.

This experience told my soul that I must go on and gain more knowledge of medicine so that I could help more people without waiting for help. Medical school was the next dream or goal that I added to my life's list.

My assignment in South Carolina ended after six months. I then went on to another assignment with Cross Country Nursing to a little town with two crossroads called Liberal, Kansas. This town was the setting for Dorothy's house in the *Wizard of Oz*.

Unfortunately, Blue Cross and Blue Shield had shut down the headquarters in West Virginia. My family continued to stay at Tommy's home as my older brother graduated from medical school and started to take his turn to help our family. Tommy traveled with me to my assignment in Kansas. The agency rented an apartment on the second floor of the building for me. I remember saying, "Awesome, we are the only two people up here." It was not until a few weeks later, when the tornados were touching down nearby, that I realized the reason why no one wanted the second-floor apartment. We had to hide ourselves in the laundry room in the basement that night. I learned about mud and hay storms while living there.

After six months of this assignment, *I knew that I would never stop dreaming. I started to pursue my next life goal.*

I applied to premedical school and went back to West Virginia University where I completed all the required courses within two years. I built up my courage and decided to take both Physic I and Physic II at the same time to avoid another semester of college. I then applied to two medical schools in West Virginia and was blessed to be accepted to both.

I chose to attend West Virginia School of Medicine. I remember my interviews for the medical school very well. The older doctor asked, "Your English is terrible; what made you think that you can finish medical school?" I remember my honest answer to him. "I have been working extra hard all my life, and all I need is someone to give me that one chance." *I had learned that a single opportunity can carry a magnificent power to change my entire life trajectory forever.* If you have an opportunity to better your life, run with it.

I married Tommy a week before leaving for medical school in the summer of 1991. We had been dating for three years. We did not have much money to spend on a wedding, but we were lucky to have our wedding at Aunt Sue's house. Several family members chipped in to buy food and rented chairs and things that we needed. My childhood skill of helping my great-aunt with sewing came in handy, and I made all my bridesmaids' dresses. I did all the decorations and made my own flower bouquets.

Tommy lived two and a half hours away because he had just gotten a job coaching soccer for junior high and high school kids. I joined my two sisters and shared an apartment with them while they were attending pharmacy school. It was not easy as my heart missed Tommy, and the wind of my emotion continued to blow against my concentration. It took constant self-talk to calm my heart and focus.

I was happy to be accepted into West Virginia University School of Medicine. I worked extra hard as my English was still limited. I remember recording my classes and listening to them several times. I did not have time to assess if medical school was easy or hard since I kept going one day at a time. I refused to quit.

Tommy would drive to see me on weekends. He reminded me often that I smelled like a cadaver from spending a lot of time in the human anatomy laboratory with my respected subject (whom I called "teacher's body") soaked in formaldehyde. I cried every time Tommy had to return home. I routinely walked to the library after Tommy drove off to surround myself with people so my soul would not cry. The spirit of studying would take over.

I was beyond happy when I graduated four years later, in 1995. I finished three more years of family medicine residency training in West Virginia before becoming who I am today. I returned to St. Francis Hospital where I had worked as a nurse. I was able to earn extra income moonlighting there as a house physician on the weekends while I was in residency training.

My brother had moved from West Virginia to Salisbury, North Carolina, and began practicing medicine in this charming, historic small town. I later joined him after finishing my residency training. I also moved my mom in with me after buying my first home in 1998 at the age of thirty-one. We soon found mom her own new home that same year.

I am forever grateful that life had taken me step-by-step from a sad, lost little girl to a woman who stands with the people who may be lost in life or hurt by love or lost hopes and dreams. This old soul of mine will forever remind people to keep on moving forward, to rediscover their lost direction, to love again with more strength, to bring back broken spirits sprinkled with hope, and never to stop dreaming in life. I continue to remind people to stay connected and never to hesitate to ask for help from your divine team, which will forever be with you and will never give up on you. Your divine team—your team of healing light—will continue to whisper directions, answers, and solutions you need. This is the "whispering of the light."

I believe that we must focus and enjoy the bliss of today during our life's journey. Our destiny will appear when it is the right time once we have captured the needed experiences and lessons from the current life chapter before moving to the next. Everything in life happens in divine timing. The universe will give us the situations, people, and things that we need before moving on to the next step of our life's journey. Sometimes you may need to just sit with patience and wait for the right time. Your divine team will work behind the scenes to bring your life and dreams into your 3D reality. So many moving parts must be coordinated in concert before your dreams can be manifested.

16

BE GRATEFUL AND GIVE BACK

All of us want the best things in life, but are we ready to give the world our best?

I go to bed with a thankful heart and awaken in the morning with the same grateful heart for all the blessings in my life. *Gratitude is a magnet for life's abundance and blessings.* The more a heart is filled with gratitude, the more the universe will bring abundance in every way—not only in material ways, but also in love, joy, and happiness.

I am grateful for the country that has given me and my family better lives. I promised myself that one day I would give back to this great nation and serve in the US military. My sister, Sas, had served for six years in the US Air Force as a pharmacist, and my cousin is still serving in the Navy as a dentist. He has been there for more than twenty years. I initially filled out an application to join during Operation Desert Storm in the 1990s, but I had to back out since my mom cried when she heard about my decision to join the military.

I called the US Navy and the US Air Force. I decided to join the Air Force since they responded to my call first. I was forty-four years old, which most people thought was rather old to join the military. I remember the recruiter on the phone asked if I could run one and half miles and perform pushups and sit-ups to pass the requirements for the standard military fitness. I said "yes" with a clear and confident voice to all of the above.

That evening I found out that my spirit was tougher than my real physical body. I asked my husband to time my pushups. My goal was to be able to do at least forty pushups in sixty seconds. My husband had his timer and said, "When are you going to start and do the first pushup?" I got up, looked confused, and said, "I could not do even one pushup today." My optimistic spirit was confident that I would train my body to reach that goal before I was to leave home for officer training school a few months later. *I learned in my life that I must continue to focus on my strength and not my weakness.* I started to do pushups on my work desk, at least ten between patients, while I was working as a family physician in the clinic. I slowly started to do pushups on the floor. After a few weeks, I was able to do fifty or more pushups in sixty seconds. I had no problem doing situps, so I began to train myself by running each morning.

During this time, unfortunately, my husband had a massive heart attack while playing soccer. Normally I would be working, but for some reason, I took time off to be at home on the day he had a heart attack. He got a ride home from the soccer field because he felt weak and fatigued while playing. He planned to come home and rest. When I saw his face, though, the physician in me told me that he looked critical. Luckily, the hospital was only two minutes away as we rushed him to the emergency room with blood pressure of 60/0 and no ability to talk or move. He did not have chest pain like other people with acute heart attacks, but after I asked further, he indicated he had chest tightness. As soon as he got to the emergency room, the quick EKG showed evidence of an acute heart attack. He received a thrombolytic therapy to dissolve blood clots in the heart arteries. He was then transferred to the heart center of another hospital in Charlotte, North Carolina, for three stents to be placed. He recovered remarkably well and was able to leave the hospital after a couple of days.

A few days before I was scheduled to leave for military training, my husband found out that he needed an emergency three-vessel heart bypass after a repeated test showed that all his stents were blocked. He also had a significant new blockage called "a widow maker." The military allowed me to stay home, so I delayed the officer school training for another six weeks to care for my husband after his open-heart surgery. He recovered well and was going for cardiac rehabilitation. He was able to stay with our good friends while I left for officer training school.

I had to hold up a folder saying "Over Forty" while going through the military entrance processing station, and I was the last one to complete my physical exam, including a twelve-lead EKG. I entered the commissioned officer training (COT) class at Maxwell Air Force Base in Montgomery, Alabama, in May 2010. It was a physically and mentally challenging course, but I made it through with great pride. I was one of the oldest among the candidates, who were mostly in their twenties.

Because of my prior career in medicine, I was commissioned as a major and had to lead other young candidates as the squadron's leader. I had no background or training before leading a squadron during COT class. I asked lots of questions, studied hard, and spent time in the bathroom reading during the lights-out time. I also sought help from the team.

I was surprised that the collective knowledge and problem-solving of my young team were beyond my imagination. Their spirits were motivated to conquer many tasks and they were hungry for adventure. They asked me if I needed a waiver to sit out from all the physical training due to my advanced age. Of course, I replied, "No, I am here to enjoy every bit of it."

I gave it my best shot with the physical training and passed all the requirements for the fitness tests except for one injury. I fell off the monkey bars one day during the exercise. When I hit the ground, the pain in my upper back took my breath away. I toughed it out and kept on going, not knowing until a few years later that I had a compression fracture of my thoracic spine from that fall.

Another thing that I discovered about myself was that I had no rhythm. There was no way for me to lead the formation during marching even though I gave it my best try. I was more than glad to give up the leading position to another young candidate (he was in the Army before) with experience, and he did a remarkable job. *I learned that nothing in life is limited if I gave it my best shot.* I also learned that I could climb the mountain and cross to another side, despite any falls, if my spirit decided that I can.

Importantly, I learned that you shouldn't hesitate to ask for help. You will be surprised how many people are willing to reach out their hands to help you, and they ask nothing in return. There are many people in the world who are true givers.

After COT class, I was stationed at Langley Air Force Base (now called Joint Base Langley-Eustis), in Hampton, Virginia, as a family physician. I was also in charge of the vaccine and allergy clinic. In addition, I was part of the Global Disaster Response Force that regularly trained together for deployment as a team. I am honored to have had the opportunity to spend four years taking care of many military families and leaders. I met many wonderful and remarkable people during my years of active duty. Many of them had sacrificed so much, not only as individuals, but as whole families.

My perception of the word "freedom" has forever changed after my four years in the service. I now understand in my heart the deep meaning of all the sacrifices and courage of many generations to uphold our rights so that people can continue to pursue the American dream. We live free today because of those brave men and women who understood that they would rather die fighting for freedom than be prisoners for life.

Once I was honored to care for one of several commanders that had passed through the Air Force base, Col. Kory Auch. I know that the divine team had directed me to take care of this beautiful soul and his family. He required hospitalization due to a significant life-threatening illness, and I had to send him back to his duty as commander per his own request. It was still too early because he was still undergoing treatment. Due to my concerns as a physician, I asked him to rest and take time for his body to recover. I still remember the selfless and altruistic words he said to me: "Sometimes your health has to come second." This way of thinking has never crossed the minds of many of us who are safely at home or even when we are recovering from our illnesses.

Those noble leaders who practice the power of sincere selflessness or have life purposes that are bigger than self will continue to be protected by the divine team. They will experience life's true fulfillment and deepest joy. Many times, our divine teams work together to protect all of us.

I dreamed about what was going on in Colonel Auch's health as if I were directed to focus on his healing. I dreamed of watching him tossing and turning and unable to sleep. The next day I asked him about that, and he replied that he did have problem with sleep that required changing his medications. He eventually required surgery, and I was asked to be present on standby during the surgery. I normally do not do this as a family physician. I was surely meant to be there, since he required an antibiotic before his large colon could be cut or resected to prevent infection due to significant bacteria loads. The usual antibiotic was getting ready to be hung, but I quickly remembered that his bowel bacteria contents were different. The normal antibiotic would not have been able to prevent the possible complication from infection. I quickly asked the team to change to the appropriate antibiotic. I was guided by my divine team working with his guiding angels to be there.

He eventually recovered well and was back to normal health after the surgery. Reconnecting with him almost ten years later, I saw that he had totally recovered.

People who take on the greatest responsibility to lead and protect others with compassion and who sacrifice their own safety and happiness will be forever protected by their divine team. I truly believe that the power from the universe will be right with these people to clear the path so they can achieve the greatest goal of protecting the collective. The most powerful forces of all the troops of the divine teams will forever stand by them.

Another important thing I have learned as a physician in the current world of evidence-based medicine is that we must not lose the ability to look at the person as a unique individual. Treatment for every illness today is protocol based, derived from research of a group of people, and it does not work all the time. Certain treatment recommendations can cause side effects or may not be helpful to a particular person. Caution and follow-up with each patient are necessary. Each life is valuable and precious. Every life is a great love to their loved ones.

Life must be cared for and saved while living. I remember arguing with doctors in the late 1990s when I kept my elderly patients' systolic blood pressure close to 150. I had noticed that they had more dizziness and falls when their systolic blood pressure was 140 or less as recommended by the guidelines then. It took another fifteen to twenty years for the new protocol to come out. This allowed patients sixty-five or older with systolic blood pressure up to 150 to be regarded as normal.

It is important to embrace every human's uniqueness and appreciate the diversities of life. The diversity of people of the world also helps us to understand ourselves better and to make this world an exciting place to explore.

All of us want the best things in life, but are we ready to give the world our best? The US Air Force's core value is "Integrity first, service before self, and excellence in all we do." This should be the core value of every living soul on this earth so that we live our lives with honor, help each other in the community, and do the right things when no one is looking.

Within a couple of weeks after I arrived at Langley Air Force Base, I received an order to be deployed with the Army to a camp at the foot of the mountains in Mazar-i-Sharif, Afghanistan. I was forty-four years old and had never touched a gun. Officer training school did not include firearm training. I had two weeks to get ready for the mission. I remember trying to get scheduled quickly for a firearm training class since I would need to be armed during this mission. In my mind, I told myself that I was ready and that I would be honored to take on this mission with my full patriotic heart.

My nerves were worked up before the firearm class. Luckily my good friend, Capt. Nick Nelson, heard about my urgent need to train quickly. He is an awesome shooter and a natural firearm instructor from his experience in the Army before he joined the Air Force. He was kind and gave his time on a weekend to help me. He got me to a shooting range outside of the base to become familiar with a Glock 19/M9. I felt that the bullet went to another part of the earth the first time I shot due to the gun's kickback in my inexperienced hands. Captain Nelson patiently said, "OK, let's put the gun down for just a second." I took some deep breaths and tried again. Luckily, the second bullet landed on the target. He got me comfortable enough for my scheduled class the next day. I remember closing my eyes every time the gun fired. The target was just too far on the hillside. For an unknown reason—or maybe beginner's luck—I qualified as an expert on my first day of the training.

My divine team knew or decided that it was not my call to go to Mazar-i-Sharif. Something happened to my security paperwork. The Army didn't want me to be deployed with them and considered me as "possible threat." My security paperwork needed more time to be completed. My deployment assignment was then given to another officer. He stated that I was ready for this mission and that my attitude had inspired him to be ready as well. After six months of this mission, he returned to base and stated that one day he might be able to talk to me about his experiences on this mission. He was glad that I did not go to this one. I was happy to see him back safely. But even today, we have not yet spoken about his experiences.

At this time I was involved in setting up standards and processes to create the US Air Force Global Disaster Respond Force at Langley. This team could be deployed and set up as a mobile hospital in a very short time in case of a world disaster or major incident. Our team got a chance to be the first to test the new EMEDS (Expeditionary Medical Support) tent in 2012 at Langley. This new tent setup required much less time when compared to the older tents.

It was then scheduled to be tested again in a real-world setting, a friendly humanitarian mission in Peru. I was excited since I've always dreamed of going on a humanitarian mission trip. At this time, I was promoted to the rank of lieutenant colonel. Our team was equipped and staffed to provide primary care, dental, orthopedic, gynecology, emergency, radiology, pharmacy, surgical, and pediatric services. I was soon deployed with this team in the remote, mountainous region of Peru. We treated an estimated 10,000 patients during Operation New Horizons.

At the end of the mission, I received a US Air Force Achievement Medal for selflessly taking care of the people of Peru and our team members during our mission at a very high altitude (13,500 feet above sea level) in the mountains of Huancavelica.

Huancavelica is considered one of the poorest cities in Peru. We traveled more than eleven hours up winding mountain roads with no safety side rails. We saw countless mountainside crosses marking deaths during prior accidents. My spirit felt safe with trust in the protection of my divine team, yet my mind kept on praying as the bus made steep turns.

We reached the city and stayed at the hotel Plaza de Armas in the center of the town. Here the town held all kinds of outdoor activities, celebrations, parades, and even one time a demonstration that ended in law enforcement using teargas to break up a heated situation.

It took us a full day to unpack boxes and assemble twenty-two rooms with a 6,300-square-foot network of medical tents that comprised the mobile hospital on a dirt soccer field.

The high altitude, with lower air pressure and lower oxygen levels, created challenges for my team members. Some soldiers developed high-altitude sickness such as pulmonary edema (fluid leaking from blood vessels in the lung tissue, causing flooding of the lungs or the air sacs). Some soldiers developed neurological symptoms due to the high-altitude effects on the brain that created symptoms like headache or lack of coordination. Our energy levels were low, since all of us had oxygen saturations in the eighties (this would require all of us to be on oxygen if we were in the hospital back in the US). Walking up stairs was harder, and my feet felt like twenty-pound weights were hanging on both of my ankles. My breathing was slightly labored as well.

I had to accompany one of my team members, MSgt. OJ Grisson, (who is half Thai and half African American), down the mountain three thousand feet to attempt to acclimate him since he started to have an unsteady gait due to the neurological effect of the high altitude. We went down to the city of Huancayo for three days and two nights. My commander, Col. Claud Hawkins, voiced his concerns about this assignment, but I didn't want more of our forces to come with us. I told him not to worry because I was from Thailand and was used to the dangers of a similar city. Our driver could not speak any English, and I made sure to learn the Spanish word *bano* for bathroom.

I remember the long hours of the ride down the mountain as we had to also drop off a few military personnel to other locations. We also spotted a dead body on the road. We did not stop to compromise our safety since we saw a couple of people on the street who could hopefully handle the situation.

We stayed in the middle of the city surrounded by multiple small shops and restaurants on narrow streets. We could see the neoclassical Huancayo Cathedral from our hotel. We tried our best to look out for our own safety and to blend in with the locals since some of their ethnic groups were of Asian descent (mainly Japanese and Chinese). The largest ethnic group in the city was also of Spanish ancestry. We knew in our hearts that we both were away from our team and our protection. We knew that we had to watch each other's back. We stayed alert and vigilant as we walked around town to find food.

We made it back up the mountain to Hauncavelica safely and reunited with our team after three days. Unfortunately, Grisson redeveloped the symptoms after being back up the mountain for eight days. He developed a massive headache accompanied by nausea, tunnel vision, dizziness, unsteady gait, and low blood pressure. He had to be evacuated and returned home to the US. Thank God that he is back to normal and is doing well currently. *We stay connected as our life experience ties the hearts of our friendship forever.*

Some team members developed dehydration from traveler's diarrhea. They required IV fluids and treatment at the hotel. One of the soldiers from security forces came to see me with abdominal pain. During my exam, I was concerned about possible acute appendicitis and quickly ran to get my colleague surgeon for help. The soldier developed acute appendicitis and required a joint effort by our team surgeon and a volunteer surgeon from another country. He had an emergency laparoscopic appendectomy. Then he was transferred to the hotel for recovery and to receive further care.

We continued taking quality care of our team members as all of us embraced togetherness in our mission goals and friendships, with open communication, appreciation for each other, and fun activities for stress reduction.

We celebrated several birthdays with delicious cakes from the local bakery. The best cake was tres leches cake from a local small coffee shop owned by a young couple. One day many of our team members were jam-packed in that small little place for the world's best tres leches cake.

The temperature was nearly freezing, and I always wore a colorful handmade Peruvian hat when I was off military duty. Colonel Hawkins asked me jokingly while we were eating why I always wore a hat. I told him I was having a bad hair day. He then said, "You have a bad hair day every day?"

I tried my best to look like the locals by wearing their locally made hat and scarf, but I was still spotted everywhere. People said, "China" or "Chinese." The indigenous people were so small, with an average height of around five feet or less. Peruvians are among the shortest people in the world. I was much taller than they were and easily spotted. We had two groups of translators since some people spoke Spanish and some spoke their indigenous language.

I could not ask for a better commander and a true leader than Col. Claude Hawkins. He led us by example. He worked as hard or harder than his team to put up the mobile hospital tent. He took care of the patients, especially a boy whose life was changed forever after having plastic surgery to correct a congenital foot deformity.

I really enjoyed and was honored to be with my roommate, Col. Kathleen Jones. We shared not only our room, but our memorable experiences. We formed a forever friendship. She refused to leave the mission despite getting sick. She always smiled and was delightful despite her health not being up to normal. I had to monitor her closely by listening to her lungs every day. I assisted her with her medications since she had developed high-altitude pulmonary edema. My reading on the research of the prevention and treatment of high-altitude sickness before the mission was useful. She continued to see patients and took breaks to wear oxygen.

The joy of doing things greater than herself somehow strengthened her spirit and sped her healing. She was determined to recover and within a couple of weeks, she returned to her normal self. This encounter of such a tough soul in my journey stays forever in my memories.

Certain tough social, mental, or physical situations affected children, including abandoned children, at the orphanage. Children who were abused affected our spirits at times. Some of our team members had to leave to take a deep breath while the tears of sadness and pain from deep within were unstoppable. *Sometimes tears are just the true language of our hearts when we are speechless.* We would watch out for each other and encourage each other to take mental and spiritual breaks.

Occasionally, we used the mountain laundry service. We discovered that all our clothes were hand washed and hung at the top of the hotel to dry. Col. Jones and I would hand wash some of our clothes ourselves and hang them in our shared room.

Each morning, for our safety, we took different routes to our medical tent in the middle of a soccer field. Since we had intel of some possible threats, the Peruvian government sent their military security force to surround the parameters of the soccer field. We had our own security forces inside the soccer field. We also had some sharpshooters watching us from surrounding mountains.

Our military team and the Peruvian military team got together for celebrations and cookouts to strengthen relationships and friendships between our countries. *We could not communicate well due to our language barrier, but all the smiles between the teams of the two countries spoke a thousand friendly words.*

We were very busy since we saw patients from dawn to dusk. The patients lined up every morning before sunrise. I would see about fifty or more patients per day with respiratory infections, arthritis, gastritis, skin infections, parasitic infections, lung infections, urinary tract infections, and liver lesions.

Our team got to know each other very well as we looked after each other. We learned to appreciate the life we had back home in the US as we observed our surroundings and the way of life on this high mountain. We also worked alongside the local volunteers who helped us translate. We formed such a bond with the friendly Peruvian people there. They were so cheerful and appreciative despite their long waits overnight in freezing temperatures as they lined up outside the soccer field to see our medical team.

Due to intel, we had to leave a few days earlier than our original schedule and return to the US. We packed up and headed down the mountain to Lima and spent some nights there before heading back to our home sweet home, the USA. I am forever honored to have been a part of this team on a friendly foreign mission. My soul will forever remember this journey of my life and all the experiences we shared together as a team. I am so proud that this team also went to assist in Africa during the Ebola outbreak soon after I finished my four-year term.

After my four years in the Air Force, I returned home to Salisbury, North Carolina, to be near my mom and Yut. I resumed my work as a civilian family physician working both at an urgent care and a family medicine clinic taking care of patients ranging in age from very young children to the very old. My heart continues to be filled with gratitude as my life has allowed me to do so much for not only myself and my family, but also for the community and people in various parts of the world.

I also volunteered to work at a local community care clinic to care for patients with no insurance. I remembered how our family in Thailand had no health care. We lost many Thai lives from preventable and treatable illnesses. I want to always care for the medical needs of others. Some of us may volunteer our hands to help mankind and to travel far to other countries. But suffering, illness, and death happen all around us. Finding a way to help our own community or communities nearby can still save lives of our fellow humans.

17

A MOTHER WHO IS A TRUE HERO AND A WARRIOR OF LIFE

Her spirit continues to stand tall and dance with the rhythm of life.

I was blessed with the chance to spend my life caring for several thousand wonderful mothers in my career as a family physician. After my mom, Jai, turned almost eighty, I decided to leave my career and devote my future to spending time with her and caring for her as best as I could. We bought her a home in 1998 when I finished my residency training. She turned it into a huge peaceful garden full of herbs, flowers, and fruit trees. She refused to move in with anyone and chose to be in the comfort of her own home surrounded by her friendly trees. She stated that this home is where she would like to spend her last days. My stepdad, who is now eighty-six years old, stays with her. Fortunately, he is still in good shape. He continues to stay active and spends most of his days in the garden.

I sold the home that I had built in 2004 and brought another smaller home ten minutes from mom to be closer. Nothing else in this world is more important than my time with my mom. Her difficult life took years from life in her 108-pound body. Lately, her heart will intermittently beat irregularly. She has a condition called atrial fibrillation, caused by a lifetime of stress and hard work. Her heart's electrical system malfunctioned. Her irregular heartbeat often becomes very rapid, causing poor blood flow, fatigue, and dizziness.

She cannot tolerate many medications and is only able to take very small doses to avoid side effects. She had a pacemaker installed to help when her heart rate drops too low. She underwent a procedure called cardiac ablation without success, which was complicated by another type of heart arrhythmia requiring the use of a defibrillator to shock her heart back into a normal rhythm. Mom once reported, "I was gone!" She had an out-of-body experience and saw her body surrounded by fire. She refused any more procedures.

Her bones have thinned, and her lower back has compression fractures. She walks with her upper body bending forward and slightly bending to her right side as her spine deformities have affected both her upper and lower spine. Her walk is slow as her ankles and knees joints are deteriorated and deformed. She has to hold on to furniture or use a cane to get around. She requires a wheelchair to shop or go places. She can no longer drive her car.

She tries to cook Thai food for all her children on her good days. One or two dishes would take her several days to prepare. The days that my mom is able to cook for us are good days. We let her cook when she can as her spirit recharges while she plays in her kitchen. We call her "the queen of the kitchen." It has been hard to see her transition from a physically strong woman to her current fragile state of health.

Her spirit never gets weak. It is filled with tremendous strength. Her spirit continues to stand tall and dance with the rhythm of life. She is happy that all of her four children own homes and have stable careers. She is no longer worried about where we are going to sleep at night. She is no longer worried if we will have food to eat each day. She has many friends from all over the world who call or message her daily to stay connected. She is a true legend as she continues to share the wisdom of her life to everyone she encounters. Her friends are from many generations as they respect her for her caring, kindness, and sincerity. Many people remember her helping hands. She used to travel everywhere to rescue anybody who needed help, including some strangers who have now become her lifelong friends. *She is an example of a virtuous mother, a true hero, a leader of earth, and a warrior of life.*

I continue to bring angel's light to her. She feels more comfort and needs no pain medication for her fractured spine. I am truly blessed to return a second time to this life with my mom as her daughter. The light of her soul continues to shine bright, warm, and beautiful.

18

APPROACHING THE FINAL JOURNEY

The change in the emotion or the light of one's soul affects every light in the whole universe.

As the COVID-19 pandemic of 2019 hit the whole world and continued to spread worldwide in 2021 and 2022, international travel or any travel was a challenge or limited. I reminisce with gratitude about my life, frequently thinking of all the life journeys I have experienced while on this earth. I finally transformed my life's failures into knowledge, wisdom, experiences, strength, abundance, and success. I continue to learn new things daily as life is all about forever learning, changing, evolving, creating, growing, expanding, experiencing, and moving forward.

The most important subject I learned was about myself. I have more clarity about who I am and what I truly want in this lifetime. As I am older, I became the center of my focus and started to put myself through more of a self-love journey. I have learned to accept myself the way I am and with more inner peace. The better I take care of myself physically, mentally, and spiritually, the more capable or useful I can be for others. The gates of my heart and soul are now more open to feel the beauty of love and life with new perspectives and with less fear. The belief in myself strengthens as long as I connect with the divine intellect or my divine team for their guidance. I no longer flood myself with self-doubt, fear, guilt, self-blame, regret, bitterness, and judgment. I am no longer spending unnecessary time providing explanations to other people about me. I am no longer afraid, hesitant, or ashamed to be me. I finally took back myself from life.

I continue to have faith as I surrender my life to my divine team, knowing in my heart that they work in my best interest. I realize that all my life's challenges were not bad luck, but life lessons and wisdom. My divine team continues to whisper answers and guidance. They continue to communicate and reassure me that I am never alone and that they are watching every step that I make. I am frequently reminded to trust and listen to my intuition closely as my divine team communicates though this inner-guidance system to lead me toward the right direction. They also remind me that my life path has already been set, steered forward and guided by them.

Please make sure to take good care of your physical and mental self. It is important to continue your life's mission with your highest strength and stamina. I continue to take care of myself well daily by eating more healthy food, improving my sleep, drinking adequate water, staying positive, practicing daily forgiveness, and staying active physically and mentally. I continue to balance my body's energy or light-force energy by taking a Himalayan salt bath weekly and exercising daily with Qi Gong. I frequently go outside barefooted on natural stone or grass. I imagine growing roots from my feet deep down to Mother Earth for a couple of minutes to ground my energy or to be connected to her. I focus on stress reduction by walking or spending time in nature connecting with trees, birds, and animals. I prepare myself and my energy daily for the upcoming assigned life purposes or missions. Please don't forget that nourishing your mind is important as well. I am selective of what I see and what I hear, since I believe that the gateway through our soul is through our vision and our hearing. I limit my exposure to certain negative media, and I avoid surrounding myself with negative people.

Spoken words are powerful. I try my best to speak positive words to myself and others. Some of you may have heard about the famous work of Dr. Masaru Emoto, who did experiments with water. He exposed glasses of water to various words, pictures, and music, then examined their frozen crystals under the microscope. The positive words, emotions, classical music, and positive prayer directed at water produced beautiful crystals. The negative words or negative intentions directed water showed ugly or disorganized crystals.[3] We have to remember that human bodies are composed of mostly water (up to 80 percent, depending on the organ). Questions were raised in the scientific community if our thoughts or intentions can affect our physical body. As a physician taking care of thousands of patients during my career, I observed that the patients with positive mindsets would do better or recover faster from their illnesses. They seemed to have more tolerance for the discomfort of the procedures and needed less medication in general. I believe that all of us collectively can lift the vibration or instill positivity in our entire earth with our positive thoughts and intentions, as our world is made up of more than 70 percent water. If we think that our homes are not only our physical homes, but that the entire earth is our home, all of us can send love to our entire earth as our hearts love our homes deeply and passionately. Conflicts around the world would be diminished if we had a mindset of unconditional or divine love. *This divine love spreads to every living thing as people understand that we are all connected by the same beautiful cosmic light. The change in the emotion or the light of one's soul affects every light in the whole universe. The positive change of one light will uplift or change the brightness of the whole universe. Understand that the one light of your soul has the power to affect the collective.*

My half-brother, Surasak, reached out from Thailand, and we spoke on the phone about my dad in 2021. I discovered that my dad had the same heart condition as mom, atrial fibrillation, complicated by a major stroke that caused weakness in his left side. My dad had refused to take any medications and would not seek medical help in the past. He underwent rehabilitation, but he continued to have residual left-side weakness. He required significant help with daily activities of living, including dressing, getting up from bed, and going to the bathroom. My other half-brother, Tom, stays with him and assists with all his needs. My dad uses a wheelchair to move around in the house.

Mom spoke to him on the phone in October 2021. He remembered mom as "mom," but he no longer remembers her real name. He remembered my name and the name of our hometown in Chiang Mai, Farharm, where he lived with us for a short time before their divorce. Mom asked him, "Would you like for me to visit you?" Dad said "Yes, I would love to see you." We then started making arrangements to make this across-the-world journey happen for these two beautiful souls to reconnect and say hello, but at the same time, say farewell.

19

THE LAST CHAPTER AND THE FINAL JOURNEY

The story will be continued since our travel plans to take mom back to Thailand has been delayed due to the COVID-19 pandemic.

We continue to live life as if every hour and every day were truly a gift. All our life's challenges have become our forever soul strengths and wisdom that is now engraved deep in our soul's memories for eternity.

My story is from part of my soul journey during this lifetime; my light will forever be with me to infinity. These soul memories will continue to play in my soul's consciousness thousands of years from now. In this lifetime, I will continue to dream, stay curious about life, create the next life chapter, and manifest life before I run out of my breath, or my wilting physical body ceases to exist. I will then once again become a light within the universe.

Epilogue and More Encouraging Words

Don't forget to stay in the creative mode and show the world the real you and what your magnificent light and soul are made of. Avoid destructive modes that cause the delay of your personal growth to speed through your life's mission or journey.

The dimension of light coexists with earth. You are never alone. Your divine or angel team is with you all the time and eager to help you reach your goals in life. You need to start or be awakened early in life to stay connected to your own guiding angels. Your decisions in life, with the guidance of your divine team, will always make a decision or create a life solution from a higher perspective. When we take the higher ground, we can truly observe our current situation objectively. You will learn with time to hear the divine answers, the whispering of the light saturated within your own intuition. Your guiding light whispers in silence. So take time daily away from all the noises of the world to listen and reflect. You must always trust your divine team and choose faith over fear.

Everything we do in life must be done with love. We must become the love that we wish to receive from others and go the extra mile to encourage the brokenhearted. When we see everything and every situation through the eyes of love, our life's journey will get lighter and easier. Love brings so much clarity and healing to our hearts and souls. I noticed that love from our own heart vibrates at a higher frequency, just like the energy of the healing angel's light. That is why love energy heals everything it touches. Love also travels distances and can occupy every space and touches every life around the world. Only the energy of love can heal the world. Love is immortal and lives forever in our hearts and souls.

I no longer have my grandparents, my Great-Uncle Infon, and some other ancestors, but their love fills that empty part of me forever.

Self-love is also critical for you to be successful in your life's mission. You must heal yourself with love before you start pouring out love for others. You are special and must know your own self-worth. You must understand that there is only one of you in this world of 7.9 billion people. Do not accept just anything from anyone who is not making you their highest priority. Stop pouring all your time and energy into someone or some situation that is not for your highest good. It is not that you are giving up on someone, but you must not give up on yourself. You still need to always fix and heal yourself and your own soul before reaching out to help others.

Your true happiness will come when you lift up others in the same way that you lift up yourself. Search for peace, harmony, and balance in everything you do, and you will find those qualities in your life. You must live life to inspire others to become successful. Be proud that you are an inspiration to those winners.

The greatest gift for our journey in life is our ability to choose. The choice to surround ourselves with people of strength and courage is up to us. We can choose not to let anyone in the world dim our inner light no matter who they are. If you have given love and light to a soul, but get only darkness back, this soul may not be ready for your light at this time, or this soul may never be ready in this lifetime.

Live life and enjoy your every breath. Your life force energy that keeps your body and soul alive in your physical body is locked within the air that you breathe. Live in the now and enjoy your every breath since you cannot change your past. Let the excitement of your future be discovered or unfold without worrying about the unknown.

When life pushes you to the edge of the cliff, you may just need to turn around and walk backward a few steps. You don't have to jump and get hurt. Your life journey is not a one-way road. Your magnificent soul can tunnel through the ground or shoot up in the sky—whatever will work at that moment of your life's journey. You can be creative and limitless in your choice of living or the direction you choose to take.

The worse thing we can do during our journeys is to put ourselves in victim mode. This is like putting time bombs in your own way to let them go off multiple times while you are alive. Your soul will have no time to rebuild or repair if you keep doing this to yourself. This is the most horrible thing you can do to your own light and being. The little pieces don't come back together well after any type of explosion. Your soul must start from scratch, and this will cause even more delays of your journey.

Be on a forever quest in the pursuit of happiness and your own dreams. You don't have to dream just one big dream. Keep adding one dream at a time and build an empire of your dreams. Even the sky is not your limit.

A broken spirit is like a broken bone. Once the pieces heal, it will be forever tougher to break! We don't learn from life unless there is a major challenge. Our eyes will be open, and we will see more clearly once we have been through the storm of life. Be grateful for life experiences even though some may knock the wind out of you. Your true authentic self will be born from the war of life. Move on to your magnificent being. If you didn't learn from this current life situation, you will have to repeat it. Once you have done much in life, your life's journey will be smooth sailing. Your spirit becomes a warrior of life. Your experienced spirit will eventually know when to put a sword up at the right moment (set healthy boundaries) and when it is time to cut out anything that doesn't serve you. Trouble won't even get a chance to invade your life because you will learn to say "no."

All of you have a life purpose. Never forget that you are also that purpose. You must continue to reconnect yourself with your inner child so that your heart stays curious about life. Your playful childhood heart will enjoy and be fascinated with the simplicity in life. Your inner child spirit will remind you to stay authentic and true to yourself. Your inner child's playful spirit will also take you back closer to nature, the source of the healing energy that your inner light needs to reset and heal. Your peaceful inner-child spirit will also keep your inner light at peace so that you can focus keenly on life's situations and hear the voice of your divine guidance. Your inner child's playful spirit will keep you singing, dancing, creating, and playing in life with joy in the *now* as if there were no tomorrow.

You must stop standing on the sidelines of life and put yourself in the game. You must take up space in this world that belongs to you and continue doing things that you are passionate about. You must go ahead without hesitation and be a joyful part of this wonderful and beautiful world and know that you are never alone. When you celebrate the accomplishments of your goals, your divine team celebrates this victory with you.

Whatever you put your powerful mind to, you can manifest in life. Whatever you seek with mighty intentions, you will find. You must stop looking for pain but seek joy as you focus on all your blessings, which you truly deserve as a human being.

Remember that a better day will always come. Let the rain wash away any sorrow. Let the wind blow away any dust of sadness before it even settles on your spirit. Let the sun chase away any darkness before it invades your light. Whatever you have sitting heavily on your spirit, let it go. You no longer must compete with the sky by making your own tears. Keep on moving forward as a child of life and never lose faith that tomorrow the sun will rise again to bring you a better day.

Once you make peace with your painful past and stop the ghost of your past from haunting you forever, your soul will gain the strength to wake up from the nightmares of life. The death from your past should not be allowed to stay alive in your future. The fear, the disappointment, or the sadness of our past can rain on and muddy the happiness that you deserve most in your present and future. Many times in life we must pause, make peace, and say goodbye to the hurt and the pain. The only thing you should keep is the lesson that it taught you. When we hold on to judgment in our hearts, our own inner life force energy gets dimmer. When we let go of judgment, our hearts can fully see the good in all people. Even more important is that once we let go of the judgment for ourselves, we will also see the good within our souls.

The same thing goes for your loved ones; their past lessons are their lessons. They became better human beings today because of their past. Stop bringing up their past and recent mistakes but see them as their strength. You must inspire and help others remain their best selves while we inspire ourselves. You must also help them to release the pain from past mistakes. You must find a reason or an opportunity often to forgive yourself, someone, or some situation. Forgiveness is the key for true healing, happiness, harmony, joy, and peace for your soul. When you forgive, the pain has no effects on your heart; it has been transformed into peace and beautiful light forever.

You are not alone in your healing journey from the past hurt or disappointment. There are no living souls alive that have not been hurt or wounded. Some of the hurts can come from the people we love the most. At times we may have to accept that the other person may not apologize or recognize their behavior or action. The painful experiences still call for you to be gentle with yourself, to understand and see the whole picture of the situation. Initiate self-love, self-healing, and self-care since those are the solutions that you can control most. You must come home to yourself or retrieve to yourself to heal. Hurt people also tend to hurt others. The situation may be their way of crying out for help, and you may end up being the one to assist them with seeking help. If people hurt you and they simply don't care, forgive them anyway. Then move on out of danger! Unfortunately, you may have to stand on the sidelines and watch some people destroy their own light.

To set your heart and mind free, you must forgive everyone and everything. You cannot move forward in your healing journey without forgiveness. It does not mean that you have to put up with or lock yourself in relationships with people or situations that hurt you. Remove yourself from all these conflicted situations with courage. Once you have experienced things or people who have hurt you, you know exactly what to avoid in your future. All of us during our lifetimes were either cheated, stabbed in the back or through the heart, lied to, left in the cold, manipulated, deceived, or robbed of something. These tough life experiences will ignite the courage and strength in you and will alert you to take back your own power. If you don't forgive them, your heart and mind will keep reliving the hurt and the pain repeatedly like a movie of life that keeps playing the horrible, hurtful, or scary parts. This will keep you in the energy of fear, anxiety, sadness, madness, or even revenge. You must continue to rise to whom you are without the interference of other people's negative energy to release who you are not. I know it is difficult to leave the situations or persons with whom you had a lot of history, but you must move on and start a new chapter of your life's journey! You may have to give certain situations to the universe or the divine teams to handle. Certain situations are not your fight.

Everything in life is about being in balance. Being human, we cannot remove all fear, anxiety, and overthinking. Don't forget that all these mental expressions can be our protection as well. We are supposed to have fear and anxiety and overthink things when we are facing conflicts. These survival emotions ignite us to find solutions to resolve the situations at risk. Having these emotions can alert and protect us from hurtful and painful circumstances. It is the overwhelming of these emotions at the wrong time that we should avoid. Don't be hard on yourselves if you are having all of these shake-up feelings. Just know that it is the time for more focus and strength to face the challenge of life. Also know that the longer you are in these emotions, the longer you are ignoring your own rescue mission.

Hippocrates was a Greek physician. He is considered one of the most outstanding figures in the history of medicine. He is referred to as the "father of medicine" in recognition of his lasting contribution to the medical field, such as the use of clinical observation and prognosis. The ancient oath of ethics, the Hippocratic Oath, is one of the most widely known of Greek medical texts attributed to Hippocrates. As a physician, I swore to this oath in 1995. The well-known phrase of the oath is "First do no harm." I believe that all of us need to have this as the first rule of life, relationships, friendships, and career. All of us are meant to walk into someone's life or situation and help them heal. All of us will make our world a better place if we see ourselves as the world's healers and continue to help other people heal so that they can rise to become the best version of themselves.

The subject of true romantic love between two lovers is the most important and complicated human emotion. We also have relationships with ourselves, everything, and everyone around us. Every school in the world should have classes to teach young children and teenagers about love and relationships. The lessons must include how to give love, how to accept love, and most important, how to love oneself. So many emotional illnesses or even physical illnesses stem from unhealthy relationships and imbalanced love. I wish we could teach young children to learn how to protect or guard their hearts. I wish all people would consciously protect their hearts and learn not to give all of it away to any situation or anyone. There must be a balance between the emotion of the heart and the logic of the mind. We must be on the lookout or on the safe side by following our hearts in a logical way, but not to the point of letting our brains talk us out of true love!

So what is true love? I am not an expert about love. I am still learning daily about this complex human emotion. In my lifetime, I have observed many elderly couples either in my own family or among my patients who fought life alongside each other until their very last breath despite the aging of their physical bodies. Beauty remains forever in the eyes of love. I continue trying to understand the qualities or the deep meaning of true love. I think the feeling of true love from the heart space occurs as a combination of the energetic sparks between the two souls that continue to communicate and vibrate in alignment at the same energetic level to experience joy and harmony. These dual vibrations continue to change, shift, and move with the wave of life. This is why two people in love have to continue trying to work together through life's challenges or crises. It is important for the two lovers to stay in the same alignment and to stay in the highest vibration of love.

The spark of love is automatic, healing, energetic, inspiring, infinite, universal, unconditional, and magical. It requires the conscious mind to hold up or live up to the highest task to keep that magical light of love shining brightly. When your heart is fully in love with someone, you know it without a doubt. It should not feel like a burden when you are truly in love with someone. The power of love tremendously energizes you to do things beyond what you could ever imagine. The vibration of love is healing and is like the healing energy of angel's light.

When your heart and soul fill with true love, you should be a better version of yourself. You should not love yourself less when you are within the bubble of true love. I picture in my mind what imbalanced love looks like. It is like the two bodies of water from the melting glaciers with fresh water and the salt water of the ocean, which refuse to mix due to different density or consistencies. This creates the fighting force when two oceans come together as in the Gulf of Alaska. This is how the energy of two souls that are not in alignment collide. People carry different meanings or perceptions of true love in their hearts depending on their life's experiences and cultures. This is the main reason why the two souls in love must continue to communicate their meaning of true love. Love asks the two souls to work together to reach that balance or middle ground.

Love is not a fairy tale. It is a continuous act or support of togetherness to overcome life's obstacles, pain, fear, or challenges without giving up or letting go of one another. Another big question to ask is does another person deserve your highest or true love? If two hearts are not in alignment for love, the magic of true love will not be able to spark or display. You cannot force love to occur. Love should not bring fear, anxiety, or sadness unless other emotions are out of alignment.

There is the danger of loving too much, especially when there is no equal give and take or when unhealthy behaviors are exhibited. This imbalance will create mental blindness, delusion, disturbance, and turmoil of our own emotions. We will feel exhausted and drained. While emptying all the healing love from our hearts to other people, we may start neglecting ourselves. Your sense of identity, self-love, and self-worth will be lost. Your self-care will cease. This can bring about jealousy, hurt, and clingy behaviors. Putting others on a pedestal or doing too much for them may encourage them to show less appreciation for you. The vitality of our soul's light depends on self-love, and it will not survive if depleted. Unconditional true love is not the same as unconditional tolerance. Most importantly, we should invest our energies in finding our true selves before we seek true love.

Don't forget that the most powerful quality you possess is your ability to choose of your own free will. Take time to choose love as the truth will always be revealed with time! The true color will always show or surface with time. As the old saying goes, "Love will stand the test of time." You must find someone who is in alignment with you or willing to grow and shift into that alignment. Don't forget that you can be happy alone. You need no one else to complete you. All you need is self-love to feel the happiness and the joy of love in this life. Don't forget that you are already the body or the vessel of true love. Once you have self-love, your vibration is higher and you will attract the one who carries that same high vibration of true love.

The task of finding, creating, supporting, and keeping up with true love is one of most challenging and difficult missions of life. Sometimes it never occurs in one's lifetime. It takes every known human skill to operate at the highest function to hold up the beauty and the shining light of true love. The required skills are not limited to skills of communication. Listening; developing faith, trust, compassion; and forgiveness are essential. Conflict resolution, avoiding judgment, loving oneself, having self-worth, being motivated, and working as a team to handle finances or other everyday situations are also valuable assets.

Many times, sacrifices are required. Allow yourself to seek opinions from experienced or wise people or from professional counselors whose skills can support or strengthen true love.

My husband of more than thirty years simply tells me that true love is when he sees me happy or when both of us feel happy doing little or big things together. We continue to inspire each other to be better versions of ourselves. My Great-Uncle Infon told me that we have been together in three past lives. We continue to learn about each other one day at a time. We still ask each other what we could do differently to help both of us feel the joy of love and life in our current lifetime.

I asked some of my family and friends to give me their meaning of true love. My little sister, Sasitorn Sukkasem, who is a doctor of pharmacy, stated that she cannot find a better explanation than 1 Corinthians 13:4–7 in the Bible.

"My take on true love is that love is forever now, at this instant," she said. "Love does not judge or keep records of wrongdoing. If you only live in the present moment, then you have no past to base your frame of reference on. Therefore, all are perfect in this instant, and we are love. Love is changeless. Love is forever now, and therefore it cannot be changed. It is perfect constantly. Love is whole. Love is not fragmented. Love means seeing everyone as part of oneness, part of you and perfect. Love is the greatest gift given to us by God. We all are here to remember the true meaning of love because that is all that we are. If each and every one of us would remember who we are and love each other like there is only this instant where time stands still, with no past, no future, and only a holy instant, then we would end all wars, all hunger, all arguments, and all suffering. It only takes one of us, and when we all look in the mirror that one of us is ourselves. Jesus said to love one another as he loves us."

My Malaysian friend, Danis Luke, a successful race horse trainer, has been married for thirty-four years, and has three children and a grandchild. He said, "Our way of true love is pretty simple. Saying I love you is so commonly used. We normally show our love not much by words, but more by action. Just asking a few things, like how was your day, and have you eaten? Helping out at home is important, doing things like hanging out clothes and watering plants. Also not taking your wife for granted. We still leave love notes under pillows, in shoes and coffee cups."

My friend, Wanda Smith, a social worker and a former coworker, said, "Love is being there 24-7 no matter what is needed. Love is actions, not words."

You have your own meaning of true love that is unique to your own heart, but don't forget to share it with the one you truly love.

Never Let Go of Beautiful Hope
A broken heart can heal.
Have no fear.
Sprinkle it with hope.
It doesn't matter how many times you fall,
Hope will get you up again.
With hope your broken wing can fly to the highest height.
As long as you never let go of beautiful hope,
Long lost dreams will come alive again.

My own soul journey of self-discovery and self-exploration is continuing alongside your journey. It is truly a wonderful life, and there is still so much for all of us to explore. Together, I hope that we will get to the very special and magical destinations that we collectively began traveling to as one light from the very moment that you began reading this book. As you read this book and we continue our soul journeys together, you have already seen your authentic self appear in front of your eyes. At this point, you have figured out more about your dreams and your goals, big and small.

You have chosen to become your own best friend and have chosen several high-quality people into the circle of your life because they are meant to be on earth for you and because they are your given soul family. At this point, you are starting to enjoy much love, kindness, and happiness—the same things you are pouring out of your heart for others. You are committed to becoming a lifelong student and a lifelong teacher. You will set a good example for the next generations and teach them the same secret or steps of life as you continue to share your soul's wisdom. At this point, you will earn love and respect from others because you have so much love and respect for yourself. You have forgiven yourself and others and have transformed the pain from your past into your greatest strength. You will see every difficult thing as a challenge, every ending as a new beginning, everything lost as a new discovery, and every darkness as the beginning of the beautiful daylight.

It is truly my honor and my privilege to walk a journey of life with you through this book. I am eternally grateful for all the incredible journeys and the countless memories imbedded in my heart and soul's memories. I hope that your destiny becomes the most incredible place, the most beautiful of all beauty, the river of all your dreams, and the fullest life you can ever live. May all of you continue to live life with the highest appreciation for it. May you collect the lessons from the most meaningful life adventures to forever strengthen and decorate your beautiful soul. May you become the bright light that forever shines love in this amazing world.

Please always know in your heart that you are magnificent. You carry the knowledge, wisdom, and life experiences of thousands of years. You are not a beginner at life. Once you realize your potential, you will be able to look deep into your soul's memories and be confident in this lifetime to accomplish all the life missions that you were sent to live as a warrior of life. Live your life well and enjoy this life's journey!

May all of you awaken your ancient soul and bring out the genius within you. May your beautiful lights carry only the wisdom from life experiences to eternity. The light in me will forever honor the light within you. Thank you for allowing me to share the story of my life.

My Great-Uncle Infon in the 1970s

Me in 2010

From left to right: My two sisters, me, and my brother. My grandparents stand behind us.

From left to right: Sasitorn Sukkasem (doctor of pharmacy); Patra Sukkasem (doctor of pharmacy); Dr. Paveena Posang (physician); and Dr. Yuthapong Sukkasem (physician) in 2019

West Virginia University, Morgantown, 1995: My brother and I graduated from medical school and my sisters graduated from pharmacy school

My brother, sisters, mom, two aunts, grandparents, cousin Dang, Great-Aunt JeenJai, and other family members on the day Aunt Sue (Dr. Sue) graduated from medical school in the 1960s

Three pictures above: My Commissioned Officer
Training (COT) class at Maxwell Air Force Base
in Montgomery, Alabama, May 2010

Promotion from major to lieutenant colonel
at Joint Base Langley-Eustis, 2012.

Me at Operation New Horizons, July 2012.
Humanitarian mission in a very high altitude (12,060
feet) in the mountains of Huancavelica, Peru

Me with my husband, Tommy Posang, on Valentine's Day 1989

Tommy and me in Chiang Mai, Thailand, 2017

My mom, Jai, and my step-dad Insorn, 2017

Aunt Somboon, Uncle Udom, my mom Jai,
Aunt Sue, Grandpa, and Grandma, 1980s

Notes

1. UrbanDictionary.com: Light worker
2. Wikipedia: Tombs of the Kings of Pontus
3. www.rexresearch.com/pdf/EmotoWater.pdf

Printed in the United States
by Baker & Taylor Publisher Services